HEARTS BENEATH
THE BADGE

Karen Solomon

Foreword by Doug Wyllie

Missing Niche Publishing

BOSTON, MA

Missing Niche Publishing
Boston, MA
www.heartsbeneaththebadge.com

Hearts Beneath the Badge/ Karen Solomon. -- 1st ed.
ISBN 978-0-9863221-0-5
Library of Congress Control Number 2014921652

Printed in the United States of America

Special Thanks To

Stephanie Babinski Brewer
Maureen Coupe-Foster
Steven Hough
Sam Ingersoll
Patty Klisiewicz MacInnes
Jeffrey McGill
Eranda Piyasena
Kristen Schogren
Rachel Solomon
Stephanie Sprague
Tina Uihlein
Angela DeRose White
Sierra Hills Photography

Contents

Foreword i

Preface... v

Acknowledgements.. x

THROUGH THE EYES OF A COP..................... 1

FRANCES.. 11

DON 19

BRIAN I... 27

STEVE 37

JEFF 47

FRANCIS... 57

TANYA... 67

DEREK 77

FRED 85

GLENN 91

ALISON 99

BETWEEN A MOTHER AND CHILD 105

SID 111

DAMIEN.. 129

DANNY 137

KEN 149

CHERYL.. 159

BRIAN E 171

PAM 177

RAY 187

WALTER.. 193

STANLEY 205

JEREMY 213

Foreword

When was the last time you read an article in your local newspaper – or saw a segment on your local six o'clock news – in which an act of police heroism was extolled? When was the last time you saw an Internet video in which a police officer did something that made you gasp in appreciation of their extraordinary skills and abilities? It's probably been a while, but not because exceptional police work is not happening – on the contrary, hundreds of heartwarming and heroic actions by police officers happen every single day. The problem is, happy stories don't sell advertising – "if it bleeds, it leads" – and awe-inspiring good deeds don't often "go viral" on social media.

While the mainstream news media continually frames law enforcement in a negative light, and anti-cop zealots devote every waking hour to bashing police officers on the Internet, the overwhelming majority of American citizens admire police officers. They are, however, a silent majority. Chances are good that unless they're connected in some way to law enforcement – they have a relative in the profession, for example – most law-abiding citizens proceed with their daily lives without thinking to commend a cop for a job well done.

Even if they do have a conscious thought of gratitude for their police heroes, most people today are just too busy to act on that and offer up a word or two of appreciation. Parents are shuttling the kids from school to soccer practice. Laborers are working multiple jobs to make ends meet. Americans are so caught up in the day-to-day challenges of modern life, they all too frequently fail to pause and give an "atta boy" to the copper who puts his or her life on the line every single day to ensure their safety. In fact, most folks are more inclined to thank the airline pilot as they deplane than they are to thank the police officer standing in line behind them at the fast food restaurant.

In a society where almost the entire public narrative on police is driven by negativism, a few notable voices of positivity do stand out. Some public figures are vocal in their support for cops, and a handful of people in the press actively seek out "good news" about LEOs.

There is even a burgeoning online community of people who support cops. I know this because for the past half dozen years, I've been honored to be welcomed into the law enforcement family as Editor in Chief of PoliceOne, the leading information and education website for police professionals. As a consequence of my position, I've heard countless stories of the humanity and the heroism of our police officers. I've had the privilege to cover myriad announcements of agencies' officer of the month awards, as well as the many ways – from charitable efforts to visiting sick kids in the local hospital – in which officers go above and beyond the job to serve their communities.

I've also come to know someone else whose unique connection to cops has given her access to similarly wonderful tales of excellence in the ranks. Karen Solomon has had a front row seat to the challenges facing our police – she's married to a cop. Having heard her husband's accounts of what he'd seen and done on tour, and then seeing the public fury against police following the officer-involved shooting in Ferguson (Mo.), Karen decided she needed to do something to right the ship of public opinion.

She began collecting stories of what is really happening in law enforcement with the aim of retelling those events so the public can see police in a positive light. These are tales of triumph and tragedy – stories of happiness and heartbreak. Each chapter is a gritty glimpse into the reality of law enforcement. Each account reveals more truth about cops than mainstream or social media has been able to – or even been willing to – tell.

Interviewing officers during her lunch hour, Karen collected stories. Many times those phone conversations involved tears on both ends of the line – it is my expectation that many people will quietly cry as they read some of the passages in *Hearts Beneath the Badge*.

Karen Solomon is to be commended for making *Hearts Beneath the Badge* a reality. You should be commended for picking it up and reading it.

Doug Wyllie

Preface

Many will say I wrote this book because I am married to a police officer. Not so. My respect for law enforcement began when I was a child. I lived in what is now called affordable housing and an officer fresh out of the academy and his family lived a few doors down. As I grew up with Dave as a role model in my life, I saw, even at a young age, the difficulty of his job. What I never saw was anything more than a man doing his job. Men and women like Dave are easy to find — you simply have to remove your preconceptions of law enforcement.

So why did I write this book? It's been a tough year for law enforcement. Actually, every year is a tough year for law enforcement. Men and women put on a badge and uniform to spend their working hours patrolling the streets. During their shift, they are spit, bled and vomited upon. They are dragged by cars, kicked, punched, stabbed, shot, and killed. They also stand by while the people they are paid to protect call them derogatory names, just inches from their faces. They are made out to be villains in the press and children are taught to fear, hate, and disrespect them.

An officer must balance politics, PTSD, training, public opinion, his or her own safety, the safety of their families, and the suicides and line-of-duty deaths of their brethren. They are supposed to be politicians, therapists, mediators, triage nurses, investigators and more. They are expected to make all the right choices, at all times, often with little time to process the unfolding events. They are held to a higher standard than in many other careers and little understanding and forgiveness is offered in return.

When their shift ends, the uniform and the badge are put away but the aftermath remains.

I think people forget that the men and women who patrol our streets are human, that they have families, and that they suffer emotional trauma from their occupation. We don't see what happens once the news cameras are shut off. We don't know what goes through the officers' minds and we don't know what it's like for their families.

Shortly after the riots in Ferguson, MO, my son came home and told me that the kids at school said that police beat up and kill people for no reason. He wanted to know who would tell his classmates such a thing. To answer his questions, I simply had to turn on the news. I didn't. That's not how or what I want him to learn.

Within the same week, a cashier saw my debit card from our local Police Department Credit Union and asked if I had family in law enforcement, I proudly stated that I did. I think that law enforcement and the military are the two most honorable professions there are. My pride quickly turned to fear as she told me exactly what she thought of law enforcement. I cried all the way home.

I didn't cry because I was ashamed or because she hurt my feelings, I cried because I couldn't believe that this is what it had come to. A complete stranger telling me what she saw on the news, as though it were Gospel, and blaming me and my family for it.

Seeing so much hate extended to all of law enforcement was troubling. It hurt my heart to read the news. Mainstream media isn't willing to take a neutral stance until all of the facts are out. Social media posts that go viral are the ones that are the most inflammatory as opposed to the ones that are most flattering. I simply couldn't understand why the loudest voices were the ones filled with so much hate. I wanted someone to stand up and say "Enough is enough!"

The only place I saw that kind of love and support were within the confines of law enforcement support groups. Not many outside these groups would listen or care. The voices of the ones that did care were drowned out by louder voices of anger. I listened to the fears of many law enforcement families and knew that someone needed to take some sort of action. That is why I wrote this book. Love is silent. Hate is loud. I don't want our love for law enforcement to be silent any longer.

This book is a simple gesture to say "Do you know who I am? I am the wife waiting to fall asleep until she hears her husband's truck pull into the driveway. I am the mother who tucks her children in and has had to answer questions such as 'Are the bad guys going to kill Papa tonight?' I am the person in front of you that purchased your meal or coffee because I can see your uniform in my rear-view mirror. I am the person in the crowd who wants to tell you that you are doing a great thing. I am the one who won't turn on the news because she is tired of seeing you crucified. I am the voice that says you aren't a murderer or bigot or dickhead, you are a good person. I am the one who respects the soldier and the law enforcement officer above all others. I am your friend."

Why would they believe me anyway? I could turn on a dime. They've seen that happen. They have a right to have a wall around them. They have a right to be afraid.

Everyone sees the flashing lights, the gun and the badge. Everyone reads the news. It's all a flash in the pan and tomorrow is a new day, a new incident to question. For you and the press, perhaps. Not for the officers.

Not for their wives, children, brothers, sisters, mothers, fathers and friends. It's never over. Every time they watch the news, read a paper or listen to the radio, their perceived shortcomings are being reinforced; even worse, their trauma is relived.

People are injured and killed every day. When Sally is killed in a drive-by shooting, everyone mourns and society protests the murder of an innocent. When Bob crashes his car into a tree while speeding, his family is consoled and a speed limit sign is erected. They get closure. When Officer Diane is shot at a traffic stop, there is silence. When Officer John is dragged by a motorist and dies as a result of his injuries, there is silence. The difference? Diane and John were wearing a blue uniform. It's expected that they will die.

Is it?

Do they not feel pain? Do they not need support? When a police officer is injured or killed, every other officer and their family walks a little slower, holds a heavier burden. It's another chink in the armor. It's one less chance they will be today's casualty but one more chance they will be tomorrow's. For those that were close to the incident, they carry the burden of the survivor.

Writing the book was easy; listening to the families was difficult. There is much more to them than what is in this book and I cried listening to so many of them. With each chapter I wrote, I fell in love with the people behind them. It wasn't hard; they are good people. They are our neighbors and friends. But, this book isn't about the sadness – it's about the things officers do every day that don't make the papers or the evening news. It's what doesn't go viral; it's what is often overlooked.

Although I suspect my biggest audience will be law enforcement families, this book isn't for them. They live it. This book is for the guy that is pissed off because he was speeding on the way to work and will now be even later, the gal who couldn't get out of a DUI so she wrongly accused the officer of misconduct, and the next person armed with a gun who thinks that killing a police officer will somehow help the world become a better place. Those are the people who need to read this book.

Finally, this book isn't a political statement, it's not a solution to race relations or police brutality, real or perceived, so please set your expectations aside. It's simply a book. It's my way of saying thank you to a community that doesn't hear those words often enough.

If one mind changes as a result, if one person is a little kinder when they are pulled over and if one person can hold their judgment before they assess the entire situation, the book will be a success.

Acknowledgements

There are three people responsible for this book: Dina Fournier, Steve Hough, and Jeff McGill. Dina often sees something in me others do not, and she convinced me to start blogging. Every little prod pushed me a little further; once the blog started, a book was inevitable. Initially, Steve and Jeff were hesitant to be featured on my blog, and if they hadn't eventually agreed there would not have been a book. Their stories motivated me to dig a little deeper into the minds of law enforcement.

When I finally set out to write a book, I planned for this to be my second book. My good friends Kim Poston, Herchel Aflleje Scruggs, Sandy Collum Sandmeyer and Ashley Gee Mikula convinced me to write this first, that I should write about the subject for which I had the most passion.

Knowing that they would hold me to it and encourage me along the way, I confided in friends – Tina Alligood Uihlein, Angela DeRose White, Dina and my blogging group. They lived up to my expectations and more.

Every time I cried at the keyboard, my husband and two boys would say, "Mum must be working on her book, she's crying again". And they let me cry, they didn't interfere and they understood how important this book is to me.

Keli Stubbs was invaluable to me, each time I drafted a chapter, she provided the preliminary edits.

Without J.J. Hensley, I would not have found my kind and patient editors Mary Sutton and Susan Helene Gottfried.

Krystin Dougherty Kahle and Sam Ingersoll showed great patience in trying to come up with cover concepts.

Scott Kahle, age 8, drew the heart for the cover.

To the friends who read, reread and offered criticism, thank you. So many people offered their help, college and high school friends, all the gals over at PoliceWives.org, and people I just met through this book – Sid Hubbs, Alyssa McVey, Diane Rosolko, Melody Wright, Tricia Switzer, Nancy Hough, Heather Ayotte, Sonya Kelly, Audrey Sander Erat, Tami Neuman, Cathryn Janka, Mary Clifford Hulbert, Jessica Gant, Amber Garcia, Miranda Pettis, Jennifer Marble, Rebecca Salomonsson, and Jesica Helgren.

A very special thank you to everyone that pushed me forward when I wasn't sure. Each time I felt like no one would care about this book, they reminded me of all the people that would.

Although some of the officers didn't want their full names or pictures shown and the names of the victims have been changed, these are all true stories.

My greatest thanks go to the men and women profiled in this book and all of their brothers and sisters around the world.

CHAPTER ONE

THROUGH THE EYES
OF A COP

You. Yes, you.
You look like a decent person.
I'm hoping you'd listen with reason
As I tell you about the story of my life,
And when I'm done, I'd like
You to give me your take
On the argument that I'm about to make.
But before I start, I ask for just one favor.
Please don't interrupt me until this is over.

You see,
When I was nothing more than a youngin' of three,
A policeman would come down by the house, and he
Would always wave a good morning to me.
Then, finally one day, he stopped on the street,
Got out of his black and white and walked up to meet
My mamma who greeted him with a nice smile.
They stood and chatted for a short while
Before the policeman came right up to me,
Shook my hand and asked if I'd be
Interested in seeing his shop

Up close and personal, through the eyes of a cop's,
To check out the cool radio, buttons and lights
And sound the siren that blared out a mite
Too loud for my little ears' liking
But yet all the same, it was more than exciting.
When he had finished showing me 'round,
He opened his trunk and in there I found
A mini squad car he had bought just for me
Of which I snatched up in absolute glee.
And as the policeman left waving goodbye,
I found myself thinking, gee whiz, what a guy
I'll bet I could be like him if I just tried.

So came the time to test my ability,
Right out of college, I joined the academy,
Underwent rigorous training of twenty-four weeks,
The mental, psychological, background, physique,
Graduated strong, proud and tall
Wearing my blue uniform, shiny badge and all
I was sworn in, took an oath to promise
To protect and serve with fairness and justice.
But in my naive young mind, little did I know
That no amount of training would be able to show
Or prepare me for the true state of the world,
With its bad and its ugly, that would make my blood
curl.

I didn't expect the amount of neglect
I'd see on the streets as I worked on my beat.
I didn't expect that I'd have to meet
The abusive, drunk father
Who couldn't be bothered
To see his kids fed.
Instead, he'd spend all his money
On himself and his boozing

Spend all day snoozing
Or worse off, brutally beating
The rest of his family,
Because all he really cares about
Is any old substance just to drown out
The responsibility of being a dad.
It's disgusting. It makes me so mad,
Just as mad as when I discovered
The no-good, negligent mother
Who left her kids alone
Because she had another
Place to go, a place to get doped,
A place to get low.
They'll be fine, she said to herself.
But no, lady, you're lying
'Cause your kids are dying tonight
After eating those drugs that you left in plain sight.

I didn't expect so much death and decay,
The shootings and homicides,
The cuttings and suicides.
The tragic message I'd have to convey
As bearer of bad news, as deliverer of dismay.
I didn't anticipate the time
I'd arrest that crackhead so high
On his drugs that he beat his girl till she died.
Or when I took in that lady who blew her fuse
When she got fed up with all the abuse
And stabbed her boyfriend multiple times
She's now behind bars for committing the crime.
I didn't expect that I'd have to hold
A child in my arms, turning so cold
From being drowned or strangled
Or her body so mangled
From a horrific accident

Though it was never meant
To happen that way, it happened
The same, it happened anyway.

I didn't expect to have to fight
With a giant standing at twice my height
And a build of three times my size.
My life would flash before my eyes
As he'd come at me with his big heavy fists
He would start so compliant that I would mistakenly
Assume it's okay
To just write him up and walk away.
I'd run his record and give him a ticket
He'd take it so calmly that I'd totally miss it
The hatred boiling up behind his eyes
The malicious thoughts forming in his mind.

The moment I'd turn to head back to my car,
He'd step out of his own and bombard
Me with a good two or three blows to the face,
Immediately I'm caught in a daze
I'd reach for my gun but I'd be too slow,
It takes me two seconds to even unstow
My piece from its holster, by that time he'd have been
Right on top of me, doing me in.
I'd finally get a hold of my gun
And manage to pump a few rounds in he who will run,
And run and run until he slumps to the ground,
Lifeless and still, no longer a sound.
Before I can even think of relaxing,
Internal affairs starts investigating,
The media and public begin criticizing
Me for shooting an unarmed man.
He was innocent, defenseless, fleeing and
I only have my word to back me up

But it's not sufficient, it's not enough.
I'm hated and scrutinized,
Condemned and despised.
And eventually, my name is cleared,
But I haven't won,
Cause the damage is done,
And people's mindsets are already geared
To hating me, and my family in blue
Because I'm "trigger-happy," so they must be too.

I didn't expect I would experience all this
Hatred, discrimination,
Such extreme miscommunication
All I wanted was to stay alive
I didn't want for anyone to die.
And by this time, guess what? I'm now "high-risk"
No one wants to work with an officer like this
Who now has a scar, a stained reputation,
For the sake of their self-preservation,
They would never, ever pick me,
'Cause obviously, I'm nothing more
Than a liability.
I never wanted to take my work home,
And I promise I've tried to face it alone,
But my problems seep through my very being.
My wife and kids have become victims seeing
A terrible man I've turned out to be,
So bitter and angry,
That's not the real me.

And yet, despite all ill will set against me,
I return to work, I'm back on duty
Because I took an oath to serve and protect,
A promise I wouldn't soon forget.
I put my life on the line; every single day, I dare

To risk everything, to risk it all - because I care.

Do you understand that I'm still human?
I make mistakes, like anyone.
I also feel, and hurt, and bleed,
I have my desires and my needs.
No, I'm not a perfect man
But please try to see that I am
Doing my best to do things right.
I need you to see the extent of my plight.

I have a family to raise and feed
Yet I use most of my time to heed
To a society who chooses to see
Nothing but blame and fault in me.
I'm sorry I seem unfriendly or uptight,
But from my experience there isn't quite
Room to let down my guard.
Thing is, with people, it's just really hard
To tell if someone's good, bad or deadly,
Either way, I've got to be ready
For worst case scenarios
Involving those who might've chose
To brutally kill a cop one day.
It's the day that I often pray
About, hoping that it'll never come
Because I'm not ready, I'm not quite done.

Look.
You won't always see what goes on inside
The stuff I conceal behind all my pride.
But I'm begging you
To seek and understand the truth
To see who I am, and not who I seem
As portrayed by the media that teems

With lies and untruths; half-truths at the best.
This is my plea, my humble request,
That you do your homework and get some insight
To shed more light on my daily fight;
The challenges that I have to face,
The consequences that I embrace,
Just so I can keep *you* safe.

Marilyn Ee

Frances Finch
Married
3 Dogs
Active since 2011
East Carolina University Police Officer
Favorite Ice Cream - Cake Batter

CHAPTER TWO

FRANCES

While Frances was deciding which career path she would choose, she worked as both a campus police officer and a reserve officer. After a while, she grew tired of waiting for bars to close on weekends to deal with shootings, gangs, stabbings, and drunks. She preferred the community policing style she had grown accustomed to as an officer at East Carolina University (ECU).

Some will say that campus police officers aren't *really* police, but the duties they perform say otherwise. Many campus police carry guns and have the same rights and responsibilities as city police officers. For example, the September 2014 log sheet for ECU shows calls for assistance and arrests for trespassing, larceny, damage to property, underage possession of alcohol, possession of marijuana, rape, kidnapping, hit and run, DWI, sexual exploitation of a minor, distribution and possession of heroin, and weapons law violations.

In addition to over 28,000 students, staff, and faculty, the campus is in the middle of a large city and the campus police jurisdiction ends just outside of campus. This means the campus police also supplement the local police force.

A rash of bike thefts on campus provided Frances with a deeper understanding of the plight of children in her patrol area. The suspects were children, and through videotaped evidence they were able to identify and interview all of those involved. What she found was troubling.

One of the 14-year-old suspects was on probation and being monitored by an electronic ankle bracelet. "It was sad, really. These kids just don't get it. No one seemed to care about them," Frances said.

Spending two weeks interviewing juveniles, coming to understand their home lives, and realizing some of them were already beyond help took an emotional toll on Frances. She gave up her work as a city reserve officer because she didn't want to "spend every day fighting people." Instead, she found herself a position where she needed to fight *for* people; for the future of the local children.

After two weeks of processing children, Frances was driving through a neighborhood she had patrolled before and found some kids sitting around instead of playing basketball, as they usually did. She pulled up next to their portable hoop and quickly found out why they weren't playing. Their ball was in pretty bad shape.

From a neighboring house, one of the mothers came out and immediately asked if her kids were behaving and did they need to move. Frances assured the woman she simply wanted to shoot hoops with the kids. Frances spent the next half hour playing basketball with a ball that barely bounced and a group of enthusiastic kids. Before long, Officer Aaron Stangland happened along and joined the fun.

While driving away, Frances choked back tears. She knew that the children she had just been playing with could very easily become the children she had been interviewing all week. This group of young children sat idle on their stoop because their basketball was flat. A simple basketball could mean the difference between life and death to these children. Without something to occupy them, they become easy targets for gangs. Frances couldn't bear the thought of arresting these kids one day, she wanted to give them something that gave them a distraction from the negative influences around them and something that gave them a connection to her. With a basketball she could make a connection that could hopefully give them confidence in her. Someone they could trust when they needed a helping hand.

As they were finishing their shift, Frances and Aaron talked about the fact that "the one thing they had to play with was in such poor condition they couldn't even use it. They just didn't have the right toys for kids their age." Frances and Aaron headed to the athletic center to see if they could round up some old practice balls for the kids.

Anyone who has ever spent any time in the South knows that athletics are as much a part of the community as the roads they drive. That's what made these balls even more special. Frances and Aaron weren't given practice balls for the kids – they were given brand new purple and gold ECU game balls. Thrilled with their treasure, Aaron and Frances headed back over to the neighborhood in the hopes of finding the children still outside. By now, it was after seven in the evening and the kids were nowhere to be found. Frances and Aaron would have to wait to hand out the new balls.

When Frances and Aaron pulled up to the corner the next day, the kids were happy to see their new friends. When they saw what the officers had brought them, they were even more excited. The children greeted them with whoops and squeals, it had been a long time since many of them had a new ball. "You mean these are the same balls the basketball team uses?!" A simple basketball meant the world to them. This was exactly what they needed to improve their games and their time outside.

On their next visit, Frances and Aaron brought the kids a new net for their hoop and an inflation kit for their balls. "Kids came out of the woodwork wanting us to teach them to inflate their old balls," Frances said. Unfortunately, the kit didn't help. Most of the balls were beyond repair, with too many holes on the outside and water on the inside. They were only able to salvage one.

Although they only saved one ball that day, they saved many hearts. The children felt respected that day, the officers had come back, they hadn't forgotten them. They would soon realize that Frances and Aaron were there to stay.

Frances and Aaron continue to stop and play with the kids as their time allows. They are learning a lot from each other: the kids are learning that the police aren't the bad guys and the police are learning that their actions can be the difference between an ankle bracelet and a life of freedom and love.

What Frances also learned that day was that when it comes to police work, things aren't always as they seem. She thought that getting away from the bar fights and the drunks would be easier for her, but it wasn't. Being around the children is much more difficult. Seeing their faces every day, some hungry, some dirty and some sad, is more than she expected. She wasn't prepared for the heartbreak of knowing there is little she can do to help these kids, that some of them will end up on the wrong side of the law.

Their innocence and the fact that they are victims of their circumstances often weighs on her. It's easy to take off the uniform but not the feelings she accumulates. She knows that everything she says and does has an impact on them; she tries very hard to make it a positive experience.

Frances and Aaron were grateful that they could help the kids, and they are glad that many of the small gestures they perform make such big impacts. For Frances, it's important that people know. Said Frances, "We do so much more than take people to jail, but no one seems to see it." That is why she stops, plays basketball and talks to the children every chance she gets. She knows that sometimes, a kind word can change the future.

Don
Married
3 Children, 2 Dogs
Active Missouri Police Officer
Favorite Ice Cream – Rocky Road

CHAPTER THREE

DON

Note: This section was written by the officer himself.

I followed a trail of blood up the concrete steps as deja vu overtook my thoughts.

I'd been here before, just a few short months ago, doing the same exact thing, following a trail of blood to an open front door. On this night, just like then, there had been a call for shots fired, the sound coming from the street.

A trail of blood, an open door and no body to be found.

Again, just like last time, the person was taken to the hospital by a friend, so we waited to hear from the hospital when they made the mandatory call about somebody coming into the emergency room with bullets in their body.

As I was checking the house for another injured or dead person, I couldn't help but notice that the house was exactly as it had been before. There was no furniture in the living room and there was trash all over the place. Paper plates with leftover food and cigarette butts littered the kitchen counter. The upstairs was where the televisions and furniture were kept. When you live in fear of drive-by shootings, upstairs is the safer place to spend most of your time.

As I was leaving the kitchen, my eyes were drawn to the floor by a cockroach scurrying over a button, the kind that you can pin to your shirt to announce things like, "I voted" or "I gave blood!" This button had a picture of Michael Brown on it and the words "Justice for Mike Brown" or some similar message around the photo.

There was something queer about the button being on this particular kitchen floor on this particular night, surrounded by roaches and drops of blood and dog shit.

I shook my head and left the house satisfied that nobody was dead or injured inside.

Just outside of Ferguson, life is going on.

The shootings and robberies and burglaries and car accidents and domestic incidents are still happening, and people are still calling for the police to come help them.

People still need our help, and we're still providing it.

I've received many messages from people around the world asking me if I'm all right, asking whether or not I've been in Ferguson. I am fine and I was up there for a little bit, though not on the front lines of the chaos. There seems to be a perception, outside of this area, that it's a war zone here, that the whole region is in shambles.

I can see how a person might think such a thing. I mean, God forbid the national media folks take their cameras outside of the immediate area where all the trouble is happening to see that life is still being lived by decent folks.

Here on the outskirts of St. Louis, I recently watched as several black kids played basketball in the street. They were the same kids I had seen playing ball several weeks ago. They were playing with a basket that had a net attached to it. That's a novelty in the city.

Several weeks ago, however, long before anyone knew who Mike Brown was, I watched as they bickered and argued and almost got into a fist fight, as young boys sometimes do, over whether or not a shot had gone through the rim or not.

"It went in," I said from the car.

"Aw, no way!" The defending boys protested.

"You need new glasses," one of the boys shouted in jest.

He was probably right, but the ball had gone through the hoop, I was sure of it.

"And you boys need a new net," I replied.

I got a call right about then and had to go. As I drove off, one of the boys asked me if I'd get them a net. I promised I would and left for my call.

A few days went by and I'd forgotten to get the net. I felt bad, so I drove around North St. Louis looking for a basketball net. Unbelievably, it's difficult to find such an item in the area where I patrol.

Poverty and crime aren't great assets for areas looking to woo businesses, so I had to venture into the County, towards Ferguson, ironically. On a Saturday morning, I finally went to a Walmart and bought several nets. I went back to where the boys had been playing and got out of my car and started to walk to the netless rim.

As I was walking towards the rim, a man in a red Camaro parked right in front of the basket put his hands out the window and said, "I ain't doin' nothin' wrong, officer. Just waitin' on my girl."

It's sad that he assumed I was headed to him, but I get why.

"I didn't say you were doing anything wrong, partner. Carry on with your day," I told the man.

Thankfully, the rim wasn't set at the 10-foot regulation height, so I could reach it without having to balance on something. I started to put the net on the rim and the guy in the Camaro got out and walked over.

"You bought that net?" he asked.

"I certainly didn't steal it," I joked. "I told the kids I would bring one a couple of weeks ago, so I'm making good on my promise."

"Aw hell, that's really cool," he said.

He came over to the rim, grabbed the other side of the net and helped me put it on. We shook hands, thanked each other and went about our days.

Later, as I watched the kids playing basketball, one of the boys asked me if I was the cop who bought the net.

"Yep. It's been a few weeks now and I'm still waiting to hear somebody say thank you." I was just being sarcastic, but I'll be damned if every last one of those little buggers didn't immediately say thank you right then and there.

I was given the honor of taking a couple of shots with a ball that had no air in it. I proceeded to chuck an air ball and what I believe is still called a brick before hanging my head in shame and leaving the kids to their game. I looked to the porch and got a smile from one of the adults, maybe one of their moms, and I smiled back. Smiles are small victories to me. They probably laughed at me, but if they did, at least they had the courtesy to wait until I left.

The boys weren't concerned with what was going on in Ferguson because they were too busy being little boys. Most of the other people I've dealt with aren't consumed by it either.

The Subway clerk was still friendly and didn't spit on my sandwich. An old woman took my hand in a parking lot and asked to pray with me. I'm not normally into such things, but in times of crisis, being open to anything can only help. She asked Jesus to lift me up and help me be just and fair and to remain safe as I do God's bidding. I don't know about all that, but I was glad for the prayer. She was the second person to ask if they could pray with me in a week. It hadn't happened, that I can remember, in the fifteen years I've done this job.

I'm still responding for calls about accidents and shootings and assaults and everything we always deal with.

Life goes on, even when there's chaos.

Crime never takes the day off, and may even become worse when there's chaos. I am responding and I am helping and I am hoping, just like I believe the citizens are, that the mess in Ferguson is resolved soon.

We hope all this violence isn't for nothing. Something has to change, and change for the better.

Shame on all of us, if we let this pass and we don't become better people for having endured it.

That'd be a real shitter. For my part, I'm going to just keep doing the best job I can.

To start, I'm going to buy a basketball and fill it with air. I'll bring it to some boys who have a basket with a net, but no air in their ball. It's a little thing, but it's something I hope will help to build trust and healing and keep them from growing up scared of the police.

It's the least I can do out here, just outside of Ferguson.

Brian Ibold
Married
3 Children, 1 Grandchild, 2 Dogs
Active Since 1991
Ohio Police Officer
Favorite Ice Cream- Mint Chocolate Chip

CHAPTER FOUR

BRIAN I

A police officer's shift is complicated and there's not a lot of down time. As the calls in their patrol area are logged, they have to prioritize and respond. If they notice something amiss or pass a car accident on the way, they may need to stop. Officers may need back-up, paperwork needs to be completed, and vehicles need to be maintained. With the growth of society there has been an increase in crime, making things even more difficult. Some shifts don't allow officers to act as counselors simply because there is not enough time. After 23 years on the job, Brian knows this and tries his best to be everything he is expected to be to everyone who expects it.

When Brian was a kid, watching the sharply dressed officers coming and going from Cincinnati's District 3 Station, he had no idea how difficult the job was. He grew up in a rough neighborhood directly across the street from the station and noted that the police always helped out, always seemed to know what they were doing. Brian wanted to be just like them, he wanted to help people.

Brian now knows that being a police officer is much more than just helping people. Over the years, he's come to describe his job as, "damn near depressing – you just see the worst." He's right. No one calls 911 to invite an officer to a barbeque, and the person who calls the station to say thanks is a rarity. They call because something terrible has happened, or is about to happen.

Brian tries to overlook this. He's known to many as a soft-hearted guy who delivers pizza to homeless people. By taking a few minutes to sit and talk with them, he's found they are regular people who lost a job or a family member, started drinking or taking drugs. Something, anything could be the catalyst, and, before you know it, your life has spiraled out of control and you've lost everything. To Brian, becoming homeless is not far-fetched. It could happen to anyone, and everyone needs a little kindness and compassion.

Knowing this, it's not surprising that Brian was nominated for Officer of the Year for an act of kindness that came naturally to him. In 2001, in an area of Cincinnati called Over the Rhine and a few months after the infamous race riots, Brian was doing what he had always done; helping the people in his patrol area.

A man named Jim was well known to the local police, he had called the police and people had called the police on him. Jim, the son of a Christian missionary, was a Sudanese refugee who lost his right leg, and his father, to violence in Sudan. After nine years in a refugee camp, he made his way to America. Unfortunately, immigrating to America was not as easy as he thought it would be.

Jim stood out in a crowd. At 6'6," missing a leg and his face covered in tribal markings, he was hard to miss. He didn't understand American culture and spoke broken English. People immediately began to take advantage of him, and he was a regular victim of assault and theft. When he wasn't the victim, he was the perpetrator. Sometimes he drank too much and became disorderly in public.

In an area where crime is as high as it was in Over the Rhine in 2001, Jim was quickly becoming another face in the crowd. Officers didn't always have time to talk to the people on their route. They were too busy moving from call to call. Luck was on its way to Jim in the form of Sergeant Brian Ibold. A chance meeting between Brian and Jim would change Jim's life forever.

In addition to delivering pizza, whenever the opportunity arose Brian would spend time talking to the people on his route to find out what was going on. He offered them a sliver of humanity on a dark night during a dark time in their lives. One night, Jim approached Brian's patrol car and Brian asked, "What can I do for you?"

Jim's answer was simple, "I'm hungry, brother. Can you just give me some food?"

That night, Brian brought Jim some McDonald's to get him through. The next day he brought Jim a feast of canned goods – tuna, vegetables, ramen noodles and other non-perishable delicacies. Brian and Jim sealed their friendship over dinner, and the two began an unlikely association which soon included two other men.

Brian got a new partner, Joe Lorenz, a rookie who had previously worked for a prosthetic company. With the help of the officer's former employer, they embarked on a mission to give Jim a new leg. The prosthetist, John Benson, had lost his leg in a car accident and knew what it was like to need a leg to feel whole. He knew that this man, who was already different from everyone else, didn't stand a chance if he couldn't stand, literally, on his own two feet. He was happy to offer his services.

Over the next few months, the officers drove Jim to and from his appointments, often after coming off a long shift. The funds for the prosthetic and the physical therapy Jim needed to go along with it were donated. Jim would never have been able to come up with the more than $8,000 needed to get a new leg. Jim eventually moved to a new state and, last Brian heard, he was guest speaking at schools, teaching children about the Sudan. More importantly, he was sober. The leg changed Jim's life.

The cynic in someone would wonder why Brian went through so much trouble for a man he didn't know, would question why he continues to deliver pizza to people on his route. But for Brian, it's simple. "I'm a Christian. Is this something I would want someone to do for me?" He said that once you get to know a person's story, you are able to see them differently. With Jim, that's all it took: knowing his story.

To help him relate to other people, Brian draws upon his personal experiences. In some cases, he's dealt with some of the same issues. He understands what it's like to grow up on the street. He knows how difficult it is for a young boy without a father figure in his life. In the short time he has to react, he tries to humanize the experience of the people he meets on patrol.

Brian knows he can't learn everything about everyone, that he can't save the world. If someone is in need of assistance, Brian is the first one to make sure they get to the right agency. But when it comes time to take down a drug dealer or stop a burglary, Brian is the first one through the door. "I'm not the tooth fairy, but I am able to separate the two. Today's police officers have to be everything, and that's a hard thing to do." He believes the police officer of the future needs to be able to balance helping the good while taking down the bad. It's a fine line to walk with high expectations.

Brian also knows that a little goodwill goes a long way. Cops can't work alone. They need the help and support of the community around them. If there comes a time when Brian needs a little information, one of the people he has connected with will be more likely to provide it. The next officer may find himself, or herself, having an easier time because they see the people in uniform as people with feelings. And, if a time ever comes when Brian is in mortal danger, away from the mainstream crowds, he will be more likely to find an ally willing to get help and offer him comfort. He won't lie alone on the cold, hard ground because he wouldn't let someone else lie there either.

"Matthew 25:40 says, 'The King will reply, I tell you the truth, whatever you did for one of the least of these brothers of mine, you did for Me.'" That is how I try to live my life, policeman or not," said Brian.

As for his family, they are proud of him. He and his wife have been together for 30 years, and it hasn't always been easy. "In this job there's no sleep; you work at night, are expected to be in court during the day, and sometimes you need to find a second job to make ends meet. It's incredibly stressful," he said.

Although his wife is very supportive, they've had some rough patches, in large part due to the demands placed on him and his family because of his job. And Brian isn't the only one in the family who is in law enforcement. His wife and daughters are as well, they aren't employed by any law enforcement department; they are in the business because they are Brian's wife and daughters. Although they haven't chosen this life, they accept the risks, challenges, and stigmas that come with Brian's job. It's just the way it is. One can't just take off the uniform; it becomes a second skin and it's with you wherever you go. The people closest to you will become partners in your job, or they will become victims of the stress it causes. Brian's wife and children have become his partners; they stand with him wherever he goes.

Steve Hough
Married
2 Children, 3 Dogs
Sworn In 1996
Retired Okaloosa County Sheriff's Deputy
Currently Training Coordinator
Favorite Ice Cream - Mint Chocolate Chip

CHAPTER FIVE

STEVE

Steve is a funny guy: funny ha-ha and funny odd. He tells it like it is and isn't afraid to offend you. It's not surprising that when I asked why he became a LEO, he admitted to being an "adrenaline junkie." No sugar coating. No family history of law enforcement, no altruism, no wanting to save the world. It was, for him, like many others, a natural extension of his military service.

Joining the Navy had taken more forethought – he admired his brother and followed in his footsteps. Steve immediately took to the structure and discipline; it was a lifestyle that fit him well. While in San Diego, he was in close contact with many law enforcement officers and saw the parallel between the military and the police. It was then he knew that when he left the armed forces, he would become a police officer.

With a starting salary of $25,000, Steve moved in with his parents and began his love affair with law enforcement. This love affair introduced him to an even greater love – his wife, Tanya. He remembers their first meeting clearly – he was on a ride with the Blue Knights and she was working at a restaurant where they had lunch. The rest, as they say, is history. They have now been married five years and have a beautiful son.

Although Tanya adjusted well to the police lifestyle, it took her some time to get used to seeing him gear up. The Marshalls Task Force required some heavy-duty protective gear in addition to the guns and cuffs Steve would need in the event a situation went south. Tanya knew there were only two ways serving a warrant could go: best case, everything goes smoothly and they all go home at the end of the shift; worst case, something goes horribly wrong and someone doesn't make it home.

What started as a normal day ended as a nightmare for everyone close to Steve. While he is in the business of catching people, some people are in the business of not getting caught. In this particular case, Steve wasn't after an ordinary citizen. The target this time was a convicted felon with warrants for kidnapping, assault with a deadly weapon, possession of ammunition and a firearm, with a little past-due child support thrown in.

On December 9, 2011, Steve was planning to attend a birthday party with his wife and some friends. First, they had to get through the workday. For Steve, that meant helping the Regional Fugitive Task Force serve a warrant. Serving a warrant is never "business as usual". Since each one is unique, officers never know what they may find. Steve's team found that there was very little cover at the location, which became even more obvious when the fugitive came out of the house firing guns from each hand until he had no bullets left. Three of those bullets found Steve – one in the face and two in the leg.

There would be no birthday cake that evening, that was certain. What wasn't immediately certain was whether or not Steve was going to live. Even Steve wasn't sure. He had pain in his legs where the bullets had hit, a searing hole in his face and he was on the ground with more blood than he cared to see pouring from his body. His immediate reaction was to be very afraid; he had no idea if he would survive this. His first thoughts were of his wife and son, and he realized he had to figure out how to survive. He quickly put all of his training to work.

In this case his training and education, including the time spent reading outside the classroom, may have saved his life. Most prominently, his studies included Tactical Combat Casualty Care (TCC): treat the casualty, prevent additional casualties and complete the mission. Words to literally live by.

After he was shot, his partners helped him to safety and completed the mission. They remembered their training and he remembered his. They all continued to breathe, that simple, yet critical, action. If you aren't breathing, you lose dexterity and you can't move. Your heart rate also goes up. You start to panic. If you are breathing, you are focused; you can think more clearly, and clear thinking is what got Steve through.

He was rushed to the hospital in the back of a police car; it would be a while before they found out that his wound was not life-threatening; a quarter inch to the side and it would have hit an artery and killed him.

Through his recovery, Steve kept his sense of humor, macabre as it was. Admittedly, it helped him win a lot of household arguments.

"Steve, I thought you were supposed to clean the bathroom?

"Must have forgotten, after all, I was shot in the face."

"You can't use that forever."

"I know, that's why I haven't mentioned my legs. When I think I've worn out the face, I'm going to blame it on getting shot in the leg."

After ten months of recovery time and undergoing the same number of surgeries, Steve was ready to pick up his badge and go back to work. He returned to work in the middle of a warrants round-up, which meant he could get right back in the thick of it without thinking too much. He put the same gear on, and went out to do the same thing he did when he got shot, with the same people.

Three years after the shooting, Steve is able to laugh at himself. But he was able to laugh at himself before the shooting, during it, and after. Nothing's changed there. Two months after the shooting, still wearing a tracheotomy tube, Steve was buying his wife a Valentine's Day card. The cashier, who happened to be an artist, told Steve that his "necklace is the most interesting thing I have ever seen."

So what has changed for Steve? The list is short, at least the one he admits to. No one survives what he did without being profoundly changed. He admits he can't play his Xbox anymore. The action of the games is too stressful and triggers subconscious fears, a reaction that is common in people who have been involved in a shooting. Drinking is also out. Steve knows that even the best of people can go down a dark road when their emotions are weakened by booze.

Each time he looks in the mirror, he will be reminded of that day. He has a new normal, a new level of acceptance. He also has a new level of patience, appreciation, and love for those closest to him. We know life is fleeting, but until we feel how quickly it can be taken from us, we take it for granted.

Until the shooting, Steve thought he was a "tactically sound guy," but now he emphasizes the importance of training. Every officer should slow down, pay attention and prepare themselves as thoroughly as possible. Every single situation is different and every one of them can go horribly wrong. At the same time, officers can't think "this could be the one" – if they did, they would go crazy. Now that he's a Training Coordinator, he's free to talk and preach to his students about safety and training all day. Sometimes they wonder how much more they'll have to hear, but for Steve it's never enough. You can never be too prepared.

"I will be able to concentrate on my true belief – training to save lives," he said. "If one life can be saved by what I write or what I teach, then I have done my job. Hopefully, I can reach the masses rather than the few; only time will tell. To me this is the good life; this is an opportunity to provide those who desire a skill set to save lives with their opportunity to learn. If you think about it, it was really the next evolution of my re-branding, so to speak; the continuation of the change which will be with me for the rest of my days, as it has been with so many before me and many more after."

If you ask Steve about that day, he will tell you he was just doing his job. In that way, he's like many other law enforcement officers. They are just trying to get through the day without getting injured so they can go home to their families. Danger comes with the job. They all know it. When people call Steve a bad-ass or a hero, he shakes his head. He had no way of knowing that a man would burst outside, a gun in each hand, and start shooting. He didn't intentionally run to the line of fire; he was serving a warrant and the situation went south. He wasn't fighting to recover so he could go back out on the street. He was fighting to get home to his wife and son.

And while it might seem surprising, given Steve's dedication to his job, he hopes his son doesn't go into law enforcement. Being in law enforcement means being away from your family. It means making sure you are always aware, you just never know who you will run into in the grocery store. The pay is not high and police officers deal with those who have a high-degree of contempt for authority on a daily basis. Steve made an interesting observation: "Being a LEO is going to be similar to being a soldier coming back from Vietnam. It's not popular, it's necessary and it will become thankless. People will dislike police officers more and more."

While Steve doesn't like to be referred to as a hero, there's something he likes even less. He likened it to a scene in *Band of Brothers*. Captain Lewis Nixon was standing aside a jeep talking when a stray bullet grazed his helmet and knocked him down. After getting up and realizing he was okay, he said to those around him, "Don't look at me like that." Steve doesn't want people to look at him like that—the look they give to someone who has faced death.

What's next for Steve? He's received a Medal of Valor, a Purple Heart, and a Congressional Badge of Honor. The awards are over, but he's found a role he loves as a Training Coordinator. His wife is happy he's off the street and his son is too young to know what happened. He continues to be invited as a guest speaker at law enforcement conferences, he's getting the hang of blogging and he's adjusting. Every day he adjusts a little more.

Being in law enforcement requires daily adjustment because officers don't know what they will see. Will it be a dead baby? A suicide victim? A charred body in a car accident? A victim of a drug overdose? Or will they have to make the biggest adjustment ever, surviving the aftermath of gunfire? Regardless of what their day brings, they keep coming back for more.

For officers like Steve, this is their daily reality. They must learn how to survive, physically and mentally. They must be mentally prepared for the aftermath in the event they are shot or they are the ones doing the shooting. They must be prepared to see the job through to completion, even in the face of fallen officers. It's the job of the police to stop the threat. Sometimes, stopping means getting a suspect into a pair of handcuffs. But sometimes stopping takes on a more serious, sobering tone.

Cynics and scoffers say that is part of the risk that police officers take and that in today's society, anyone could get shot at any time. That may be true, but the odds of injury go up when it's your job to stop the people with the guns from roaming the streets.

As Steve will tell you, nothing, or at least very little, about police work can be called "easy." In a given shift, a police officer may have to take down a large man strung out on crack, mushrooms or the drug of the day. First responders—police, firemen, and EMTS—are regularly faced with scenes of dead bodies and horrific abuse. It's not easy building an internal defense so the images swirling in your mind don't drive you mad.

Most of us know what's on the other side of the office door. We live in a world of relative safety and security, where images of violence are the province of the TV news. It isn't part of our daily reality.

Thanks to Steve and other people like him.

Jeffrey McGill
Married
4 Children
Sworn In 1999
Retired Okaloosa County Sheriff's Deputy
Currently Training Coordinator
Favorite Ice Cream – Moose Tracks

CHAPTER SIX

JEFF

For every good guy with a gun, there are friends, family and often partners beside them. Jeff and Steve had been partners for 12 years at the time of the shooting. Their partnership lasted longer than some marriages. Some would even argue that they are married. As a police officer, your partner becomes a very important part of your entire life. A police partner isn't your typical co-worker. It's not a send memos back and forth, grab lunch and maybe work on a project together sort of relationship. Partners are there to protect each other, be each other's eyes and ears, and be a sounding board for dealing with situations that the general public doesn't understand. Your partner becomes one of your best friends, and can be your most important ally when you put on your uniform.

For Steve, Jeff was the partner who tried to keep everything, and everyone, together after the shooting. To an outsider, Jeff seems like a regular guy, hangs out with his family, enjoys a day at the beach and grabs lunch with his wife. But appearances are deceiving. Being a police officer doesn't always allow him the luxury of being "a regular guy." Being shot at more than once reduces the likelihood that he will ever be "a regular guy." Nothing will ever be as simple as hanging out at the beach again.

In 2006, a woman decided to take aim at Jeff's head while he was on duty. Fortunately, she missed. It's one thing to feel like you have target on your back because you wear blue. It's another for someone to confirm that fear. For Jeff, getting shot at was part of the job. He dealt with it, shook it off, and moved on.

Watching his best friend get shot in the face from 50 feet away was another story. He was looking directly at Steve when his face shattered from the bullet and blood "ran out like a kitchen faucet."

Jeff's training taught him to neutralize the subject immediately. He was able to come up from behind, but not before the subject was felled by bullets from other officers. For what seemed an eternity, Jeff was unable to reach Steve because there was a SWAT team and flying bullets between them. When he made it to Steve's side, Steve was alert and conscious. Jeff's training had taught him that, after a shooting, this was a good sign, despite the large amounts of blood.

Although the training was telling him one thing, Steve's behavior was telling him another. Steve began handing Jeff his personal belongings and telling Jeff the words Steve wanted his family to hear if he didn't make it. Jeff suddenly realized that his training taught him what to do if *he* were hit, not what to do when he was the officer left standing. Jeff had always pictured himself as the one injured, not the other way around. How would he keep the pieces together?

While Steve was life-flighted to a trauma center, other officers picked up Steve's wife, Tanya, and let her know Steve had been shot. Jeff was left to drive to the trauma center alone. His mind was working overtime wondering how he would deal with the aftermath. The trauma was so intense that he doesn't remember much about the discussions he had or the comfort he received. He does remember the nurse handing him Steve's wedding ring and belongings before Tanya arrived so he could give them to her.

When Tanya arrived, Jeff felt like he had been lying too much already – assuring Steve that he didn't look that bad and that he was sure Steve would be just fine. After all that, he had to look Tanya in the eye and prepare her for what she was about to see – without lying. While dealing with his own shock and sadness, Jeff constantly shifted positions so no one else would see the hole in Steve's face. Even in the immediate aftermath, he was trying to protect Steve and his family. Neither one of them had been prepared for this. Both of them were wondering what was next.

Luckily, Jeff never had to deliver the ring or say the words. Steve was able to put it back on his finger and Tanya didn't need to put it in a box or wear it on a chain.

Physically, Steve recovered. But there are parts of the three of them—Steve, Jeff, and Tanya—that will never be the same. The uniform, the badge, and the vest are disposable. The men and women who wear them aren't and neither are their families and loved ones.

Behind every badge is a living breathing being. Behind them are even more beings – tiny beings that expect their parents to pick them up when they fall. The families that officers represent are too often collateral damage when the officer gets hurt during a crime. Their lives can be torn apart. They know that. Recovering from a shooting is never easy; recovering from a shooting and going back out to do your job, knowing you could be on the receiving end of a shooting again? That takes a special kind of courage and dedication, on the part of the officer and his family.

While Jeff wasn't physically injured, his burden, though different, was just as heavy. For him, it was the burden of the survivor.

After the shooting, he was told it was a "good" night, that they all got to go home. Did they? Not right away, not intact, and certainly not as the same men they were before. It wasn't a "good" night. Someone was shot. Something went wrong. In some ways, the best outcome was that something could be learned to prevent this from happening again.

When Jeff returned to work a week later, the desk across from him was empty. Steve's mug no longer stared back at him the way it had for years. It was a constant, painful reminder of that night. If Steve had not survived, Jeff would have handed in his badge. The burden would have been too heavy.

It is said that it is more painful to see people you love in pain than it is to be in pain yourself. For Jeff, this was true. He was angry that day, angry that he didn't kill the shooter who nearly killed his friend. Angry that his friend was shot; it felt personal. Why would someone shoot Steve?

He was angry knowing that his family was disrupted forever. They were no longer safe, and someone would have to tell their wives and kids. They were targets today. They probably will be again. Jeff can't take that burden away from his family. They carry it now with him. Nothing could prepare them for that.

We hear the term "aftermath", but what does it mean? For people like Jeff, it means that there are few who understand the world you now live in. You draw closer to men and women who have been involved in a shooting. You wonder if you can survive and function should it happen again. You compartmentalize and you come out on the other side. You also wonder how your experience can help others, how you can prepare someone for a shooting, or worse, a death.

In Jeff's case, a teaching opportunity was presented and he took it. The shift in his career wasn't because he couldn't carry a gun and serve warrants anymore. He would and he did. But since he was finishing his Master's Degree, and he had an opportunity to help other officers stay safe and cope, it was the right time for a change. Jeff took a position with the Law Enforcement Academy and is using his experience to help fellow officers. Perhaps it's a bit of therapy as well. Knowing that he may help save someone eases the trauma of seeing Steve nearly die.

There was plenty of PTSD to go around. While Jeff drove to the trauma center alone after the shooting, he felt powerless. He couldn't help, he couldn't drive any faster and he couldn't rewind time. Imagine driving in your car alone, hitting some traffic and panicking, feeling an anxiety attack coming on. Why? Because your subconscious is replaying that car trip in your head without you even knowing it. Small things like that can be a reminder of that day. Nightmares. Trouble sleeping. All of it. Policemen are not immune. You can turn off the news and assume they get up the next morning unscathed. They don't.

Was this interview a cathartic experience for Jeff? Maybe, maybe not. Perhaps Jeff just wanted to share what happened in the hopes that it would open some eyes, promote a little more tolerance and forgiveness and help someone who is going through the same thing.

At age 38, Jeff's been through a lot. Multiple shootings, marriage, parenthood and life in general. Not coming from a law enforcement family, some would wonder where his dedication comes from. The heart. It's as simple as that. He's solid, steady, and loves his family.

Nice quiet home with a daughter receiving her associate's degree and high school diploma simultaneously, a fabulous stepson and a mini-Mia Hamm. He heads out into chaos every day not knowing what it will bring. He chose the least popular path.

He doesn't see himself as a hero, a bad ass or a rock star. He doesn't like or want awards or accolades. To him, he's doing a job. People have a hard time seeing that. People want superheroes, but they are only in the movies. Jeff doesn't have a cape, a Batmobile or a bullet-proof chest. Heck, he doesn't even have his old Mustang anymore.

Jeff joined the military at 18 because he thought it would be fun and exciting. After that, he joined a street crimes unit that enabled him to do all the tough things you didn't see on *Adam-12*. He got more than his share of excitement.

In December, he'll finish his Master's Degree; his kids are growing up and he'll be keeping his wife busy so she doesn't worry about where the kids are. In the meantime, he is trying to figure out how to teach someone to cope with a shooting. How can he make it real enough so that they will understand and be better prepared than he was? How can he help them understand how it will affect their families and their future?

What he can say is the best therapy is getting help from the people who have been there. Learn about PTSD and know it will happen. If the next call out after the shooting is at the same time of day, in the same weather and no one answers the knock on the door, you will relive every moment of the last call. You need to be prepared for that. It won't hurt to have a list of available resources. The department may not be ready for what is needed, so you must be prepared. When the shift is over, you will go home alone in more ways than one. Be ready. Odds are you won't be in an officer-involved shooting, but never say never. You are your most important asset. You need to wake up the next day and continue life. Your family will still need you. Make sure you can still be there.

Francis Bailey McGill
Married
4 Children
Wife of Jeffrey McGill
Favorite Ice Cream – Moose Tracks

CHAPTER SEVEN

FRANCIS

They say opposites attract, in Jeff's instance, they may be right. His wife Francis is chatty, cute, sweet and much more transparent than Jeff.

Where was Francis while Jeff and Steve's story was happening? Out saving lives herself. Francis is a paramedic. Her personality, cute and sweet, makes for a good bedside manner. Unfortunately, it doesn't keep a crisis from striking a family.

While Jeff and Steve were in another county serving warrants, Francis was in the midst of a 24-hour shift on her way to a nursing home. As she was getting out of the truck, she answered a blocked call (something she normally wouldn't do). It was her then-boyfriend. Jeff called to tell her Steve had been shot, he was bleeding badly, he loved her and he'd call her when he had more news. Francis hung up the phone, entered the nursing home and began treating her patient.

There is always a little lag time before your brain processes devastating news, that's exactly what happened to Francis. While taking her patient's vitals, she suddenly realized she needed to be with Jeff, Steve and Steve's wife, Tanya. Her family was in trouble.

Like any other first responder, Francis put her patient first. She did what she needed to do, took the patient to the hospital, and took the truck out of service. She had a hospital of her own to get to. It was a 50-minute drive. During those 50 minutes, she had an update from Jeff with more details of the incident and she had a lot of time to worry about what was waiting for her when she arrived. It's a scene we all hope we see only on television. A sea of blue uniforms waiting for news, a show of support for one of their own. Sadness, tension and compassion on the faces of the men and women who hope to never be caught by the bullet of a desperate man.

Once Francis made her way through the group, she went straight to Jeff and embraced him. Tanya came from beyond the curtain and hugged her as well. Being an EMT gave Francis an edge that may or may not have been helpful; she saw the medical aspect of what was going on. Steve had an endotracheal tube, not a good sign; she looked at the monitor, is he getting enough oxygen; vital signs, is he stable? That is what Francis saw before she saw the wound. Before she saw her friend. Before she saw what could have been the end of what they knew and loved.

In the ICU waiting room, people began telling "Steve Stories." Remember when Steve... those stories. The stories that say he might not make it. These are the times an officer looks around and wonders if it's worth it. If your time is cut short by a bullet, will your friends have enough stories to tell? Will they think your sacrifice was worth the ending?

The stories kept everyone together and intact while they waited for news. Finally, sometime between two and four in the morning, they were satisfied that Steve would be okay while they got some sleep. But who could sleep? They had cried, watched Steve write "Tell everyone on Facebook I am going to be ok," and tried to hold each other up. Steak and Shake was still open and they had more Steve stories to tell. By seven, they learned Steve was asking for Jeff and they headed back to the hospital. That's when Francis saw the first sign of what she didn't realize was going to be a battle with PTSD and a test of her relationship with Jeff.

Jeff snapped at Francis. At first, Francis tried to be understanding. Everyone gets stressed and short with others at times. Given the circumstances, Jeff had every right to be tense. And he was angry, very angry. He saw the events as an attack on his family. Additionally, he had Steve's blood on him. He had been looking right at Steve's face when the bullet hit him. Jeff held his friend while he bled. He still didn't know what the outcome would be.

While Jeff was processing his emotions, Francis was looking at it from a cold, clinical medical perspective. Steve's leg was through-and-through and the bullet hit the jaw, not the brain. From her angle, things looked good. Steve was going to be okay, they could surprise Tanya and Steve by decorating their house for Christmas, coordinate the purchase of gifts and visit their friends daily to help with the healing.

For Jeff, things weren't that simple. He couldn't shake it, he had trouble sleeping and he was frustrated.

Relationships are hard enough, throwing a traumatic event into one makes things a lot harder. Jeff tried to talk, Francis tried to listen. It is sometimes hard for others to just listen, Francis was no different. She offered advice, she inadvertently cut him off and did everything she thought she should do.

But rather than making things better, she felt like she was making things worse. What Jeff needed wasn't what she was offering. There was a disconnect between them based on experience, behaviors adopted through their jobs, and simply being male and female. Nothing seemed to work and it took a toll on their relationship. The only thing they appeared to have in common while coping with the situation and what came after was that neither of them recognized PTSD. Neither of them had enough training or understanding to help them make their way through without hurting the other.

Jeff and Francis had never dealt with this kind of stress as a couple. And while Jeff didn't get shot, his partner did, while Jeff watched the action play out, and Jeff himself was in the middle of the cross-fire. That took a toll on him and the people who loved him. Jeff dealt as best he could, while Francis was trying to support and understand what he was going through—all while trying to manage her own feelings. Sleeping was difficult, crying was frequent and knowing she couldn't take away anyone's pain was unbearable.

Compounding the frustration was that Jeff's way of communicating was not Francis' way. He tried to talk, she tried to listen, but they often ended up arguing. She tried everything she knew to comfort him but it wasn't what he needed at the time. Her grief was made deeper by the fact that she felt she was making things worse for Jeff. Deliberately or not, Jeff was pushing Francis away and she was trying to hold them together. It was a perfect formula for discord.

In addition to their own feelings, they had children to consider. These children had to face the fact that Uncle Steve was shot and Dad was there. Dad could have been shot. Each child had his or her own way of dealing, from hiding feelings to being openly affected.

Not all police departments are set up to handle the aftermath of a shooting. Contrary to popular belief, it's not part of an officer's job to shoot or get shot. As a result, resources tend to be scarce and there is a long-held perception that police are weak if they can't handle it.

Add it all together, and it becomes quite the balancing act, for Francis and for all of them.

Francis and Jeff are now happily married and have been able to move past the incident. It has made them stronger and has taught them a lot. All four of them learned: Steve, Tanya, Jeff and Francis. Steve and Jeff use much of their knowledge in their new roles training recruits. There is much to learn aside from the mechanics of police work, things people don't see. It's the emotion of those involved. Francis was able to articulate that emotion quite well when I spoke to her.

As an EMT, Francis is trained to see certain things. She saw Steve's vitals, his tubes and that he would probably pull through. But what she also saw was a man, a friend, a husband, an uncle and a partner lying in a hospital bed. Has she seen this before? Yes, but this time it was someone she loved. That makes a world of difference. It also makes a difference that there were so many bullets flying that day, any one of them could have hit Jeff. Imagine your husband goes out for drinks with a friend. They part ways and a car hits the friend while he's crossing the street. Yes, it could have been your husband, had he crossed with his friend. Yes, he could get hit anytime he crosses the street. For the ones who love police officers, those bullets are aiming for them. It's not an accident or a fluke. It's very different. Guns are intentionally pointed at them on a regular basis. What happened that night with Steve is added to the fact that someone aimed at Jeff's head in a previous situation and missed. He and Francis now have two incidents under their belts that cause a lot of heartache and fear.

Recent statistics have shown that three out of five law enforcement marriages end in divorce and that police officers commit suicide at a higher rate than the national average. Incidents like these may or may not contribute to the problem.

Francis is still scared, and she has spent many hours crying since that night. When she saw Steve, she cried. She cried and held his toe at the foot of the bed, her way of letting him know she was there. She cried for Tanya and their son, her heart ached for what could have been. While she held on to the fact that Steve would be okay, she could not simultaneously let go of the fact that death just got a little closer to their door. She knew that things could have gone much worse. She knew that Steve, Jeff and their unit were well-trained, knew each other and were the best of the best. She knew that they would be okay physically.

But that is only surface logic. Deep in her heart what was she feeling? That's tough to say. How do you put into words the anguish that a pain like this brings? This isn't an illness, this isn't an accident, this is someone intentionally trying to kill the people you love. Once the monitors are gone and the flesh wounds are closed, the memory and the fear remain. What happens next time?

Before they could figure out next time, they had to get through this time. And that takes a new level of patience and understanding.

Francis is as a person who loves love. She loves her family and her friends, she loves to love people and she wants the best for everyone. Truly. Now she was being crushed beneath the weight of everything that happened and trying desperately to heal everyone. Could be the paramedic in her; could just be her love.

Regardless of what it was, her steadfast love and devotion to Jeff was enough to carry them through. They both learned about PTSD and how to help each other. They've been together five years and have four kids between them – two boys and two girls. They met on a blind date, a date set up by Steve. Some would say Jeff and Francis are married, others would say Jeff and Steve are married. Sometimes it hard to tell with law enforcement partners.

Speaking of partners, Jeff and Steve are still together teaching new recruits at a law enforcement academy. One would think this would be an easier job, a relief from the pressure and a step out of harm's way. But that's the funny thing about these kinds of events, they are never far from your mind.

It is never far from Francis' mind. Although she knows that Jeff is in a safer place, she still has many fears. He hands loaded guns to recruits on a regular basis, what's to stop them from turning on their instructor and the other recruits? What if someone targets the campus and opens fire? Jeff will be right there in the front lines, once again stopping the bad guy and protecting his friends. Francis has accepted this; this is her new normal. Worrying about the 'what if'.

She's not angry, she's not bitter, she's just a woman who loves a man who is good at his job. A man who loves what he does and doesn't want to give it up, despite the risks. This is how law enforcement families function – they live, they love and they hope they don't ever get that phone call. They accept the risks because they know that some things are more important than being complacent.

In the end, they struggled through, and it was a struggle. Jeff and Francis can count themselves among the lucky; their relationship withstood one of the toughest things any law enforcement family will have to face. They will be okay.

Tanya Hough
Married
2 Children, 3 Dogs
Wife of Steven Hough
Favorite Ice Cream – Chocolate & Peanut Butter

CHAPTER EIGHT

TANYA

You text your husband to confirm your plans to go to a friend's birthday dinner. You don't hear back, but you're okay with that because he is out serving a warrant in another county.

You return from lunch and a co-worker hands you a note asking you to call the sheriff's office joking, "You're not above the law."

You call your mother-in-law because you can't reach your husband, your son is there, perhaps he is having lunch with him.

She answers and you can hear your brothers-in-law in the background. "Is everything okay?" you ask.

"No."

"Do I need to come home?"

"Yes."

By the time you reach the elevator, you are shaking. When you reach the lobby there are two officers.

"Are you looking for me?" you ask.

"Yes. Steve's been shot in the face."

"Is anyone else hurt?"

"We don't know."

The few minutes it takes you to get Jeff, Steve's partner, on the phone are the longest minutes of your life. You are scared, uncertain and alone. You are riding in a patrol car. If you had your way it would be because you'd been arrested, not because the man you love has been shot. Telling him you'd been arrested would be a lot easier than what is actually happening. This is the ride that every person who loves someone in law enforcement dreads.

When you get Jeff on the phone, he sounds shaky but confident – Steve is conscious. Jeff is also alone and on his way to the trauma center where Steve had been life-flighted.

Now you worry about how Steve's family will get to the hospital; are they okay to drive? And what about your son? Luckily, your mother is in town and she will watch him. You call her to tell her what is going on. You don't look at your phone again for the rest of the night. The only thing you will focus on is Steve.

When you reach the trauma center, you see many other officers waiting. Waiting for news. They look at you with sadness, disbelief, fear and relief. As you rush in, you pray you aren't too late; you pray that he stayed alive long enough to say goodbye to you; for you to say goodbye to him.

Jeff takes your hand and gives you Steve's wedding ring, warm from the heat of Jeff's palm. Jeff holds your hand and doesn't let go until Steve's parents arrive.

You need that hand, that strength, that love, because you don't know what you are about to find. When you see Steve, you breathe a sigh of relief...until he turns his head. There is a hole in his face and he doesn't look good.

As if he could feel your heart stumble, he writes a note on a white board to tell you he is okay.

You wait while he is in surgery, you see the looks on the faces of people you love, trying to keep it together. You spend a week in a hotel room an hour from home, while your 15-month-old son is cared for by his grandparents.

But you won't cry. You have prepared yourself for this day for so long that the tears simply won't come. It's as though you need to be strong for everyone around you. For the family and friends who love Steve, for your son, for Steve's partner, for all the officers who are fearful they might be next. They will cry for you. You can keep yourself composed. That is the only way you will make it through. Don't cry.

Everyone else will cry. They will cry because they were all shot that day. There were twelve of them at the scene. They all felt the bullets. They and their loved ones now have invisible injuries. The dominoes have fallen and you are the one at the head of the line. You refuse to fall.

Tanya is Steve's wife, and this was her day – December 9, 2011. You all know by now that, thankfully, Steve survived.

Finding a way to cope in the aftermath of a potential tragedy is important for everyone involved. Being the wife of an officer who has been shot isn't easy. It's a huge burden; everyone is looking to her. Is she okay? Can she deal with the press, the accolades and the investigations to come? Will their relationship survive? Will she make it easier for us to deal with our own feelings, or will she make it more difficult?

For Tanya, the natural thing to do was focus on Steve. Blocking out everything, and everyone, else was the smartest thing she did.

No matter how many times you watch someone put on their uniform and Kevlar vest, you are never prepared for a shooting. It was always in the back of Tanya's mind, but she never quite believed it was going to happen. Warrant-serving officers seem to be favorite targets of lunatics with guns. Steve and his team fit the bill perfectly. In hindsight, Tanya realizes it was inevitable that one of them would go down.

She had a lot of time to think about all of this as she sat by his bed, day and night, while he was in the hospital. She took only the briefest of breaks to see her son. Luckily, Jaxon was too young to understand what was going on. Someday he will know the story, but not yet. Tanya is barely getting over it herself.

The hospital offered Tanya and Steve comfort, safety, and a refuge from the media. Much too soon it was time to go home, and that was when reality set in for Tanya. As she was taught to care for Steve and his wounds, her primary thought was "Are you (insert random expletive here) kidding me? You saved him only to send him home with me? If he chokes I probably won't cut the wires quick enough to save him or I'll give him an infection and kill him!" But off they went, Steve thinking his loving wife was going to care for him, her thinking she was going to kill him. With an emotional escort of police cars taking them home, the comfort of the hospital was gone.

With the loss of that comfort, the real world seeped in. She had pockets full of business cards from people she had never met before. All of them had assured her they would do anything they could to help. But how could they help? How could these strangers mend the hole in their lives? Steve and Tanya had to hold onto each other and try to make it past their fear, grief, nightmares and the sudden feeling that they were living inside a cracked snow globe and their sanity was seeping out.

Steve became angry and short-tempered, and there was enough physical and emotional pain to drive them both mad. But they hung on. Steve was pretty self-aware; he knew he was having problems and needed to deal with them before they took down his family. They sought counseling, and Steve was able to write and get his feelings onto paper while Tanya watched and waited. She knew someone had to be the anchor in the madness.

She listened a lot and asked questions in an effort to get him to reveal more, to get it all out. She knew that he couldn't keep it in – it would eat him alive. By the end of the first month after the shooting, Steve was strong enough that he wanted to visit the crime scene. They met up with some of the team and headed over.

It was a difficult, emotional time. Exiting the car as if in slow motion, standing on the ground where a gun-fight took place just a few weeks ago; the location where Steve could have taken his last breath. Though the shell casings were long gone, the bullet holes remained. The smell of gunpowder was no longer in the air, but the smell of terror remained. It was time to move forward with the healing process.

Tanya spent months nursing Steve through numerous surgeries, caring for their son, and managing well-wishers and the media. She also had to manage the fact that some people disappeared from their lives; perhaps it was too much for them. Rather than build a silent resentment against the people who couldn't contain their own emotions long enough to offer her support, she focused on the good: the love in their lives and the fact that Steve was still alive.

For Tanya, the most important thing was moving through the fear, trying not to let it get the best of her. She had to focus on what was right and good, and that was that Steve was still with her. It took a long time to look at him without having a sinking feeling in her stomach. It took even longer for the anger to pass – anger at people who shoot other people without reason and with complete disregard for the families that are waiting for them at home.

What was most important for Steve was getting back into the thick of things, and Tanya let him go. Despite her fears, she knew he needed to go on a full warrant sweep his first day back. Was she filled with dread? Of course. But she knew Steve as a noble man, valuable to his team and someone who would use his incident to teach others how to survive. And that is exactly what he is doing now.

While Tanya is breathing a little easier today, it wasn't easy getting here. She feels a sense of relief that Steve no longer has a target on him. The target of a badge on his chest. If he doesn't text back immediately, or answer his phone, she freaks out just a tiny bit until she gets Steve's tactful response of "still alive." He is such a card.

The two-year anniversary of Steve's shooting was a difficult one. Tanya has learned that lightning does strike twice. Their nephew, by Steve's oldest brother, barely survived a car accident only to be killed in a second accident two years and two days after the first one. Although Steve hasn't been shot again, his face, his job, and the simple act of getting up in the morning are constant reminders of a tragedy avoided.

Derek Gray
Married
1 Child, 1 Dog, 2 Cats
Active Since 2011
Kansas Police Officer
Favorite Ice Cream – Chocolate Malted Crunch

CHAPTER NINE

DEREK

At 30 years of age, Derek has done a lot. He's spent ten years in the Army. During four of those years he was an EMT and a volunteer fireman. Now, he is a full-time police officer. With parents in law enforcement, it's not surprising that Derek found his way there, eventually. Although he enjoyed the military, deployments were difficult and traumatic. Derek found himself searching for a way to make a difference in his own community. With one year of active duty left, he decided to become a volunteer police officer.

Similar to a volunteer fireman, Kansas once had volunteer policemen. The counties didn't have enough money to pay for enough law enforcement, so they supplemented their skeleton crews with volunteers. These men and women, while unpaid, had the same powers as a paid officer. Many of these officers had full-time jobs and didn't want to take the salary cut of a full-time position, but still wanted to help their community increase its safety. Others volunteered as a way to get their foot in the door. Paying positions were difficult to come by in their area and it was best if they were invested in the position while waiting for something to open up.

For Derek, volunteering was a way of getting his foot in the door. He had come to love police work. He volunteered a few nights a week and weekends, and decided to go to the police academy. His spare time was split between the academy and the volunteer force.

In a city of 5,000 residents, one officer on duty at all times doesn't seem like much. It's not. It can be dangerous, because when assistance is needed there is no back-up readily available. The officers need to wait for a response or rely on the assistance of a nearby citizen. Two days after Derek graduated from the academy, he not only happened to have another officer with him, but he was also lucky enough to have a willing civilian nearby. Because of that, they were able to save a life.

Derek arrived for his shift expecting a quiet night. During the day-shift officer's briefing, that changed. A call came in: a woman had fallen into a fast-flowing river and was in danger of being swept away. Both officers responded quickly and were at the riverbank in a matter of minutes. They arrived to find there was no woman in the river. It was a nine-year-old girl.

Amy and her sixteen-year-old sister, Kate, had been playing near the riverbank when they fell in. Kate was strong enough to pull herself out and call for help. Amy was stuck behind a fallen tree branch and was barely hanging on. Initially, the officers thought they could throw a flotation device out to Amy and pull her in. Because she was becoming weaker by the moment and the river was flowing quickly, they knew that even if they could get it to her, her strength would be sapped. The risk Amy would not be able to aid in her own rescue was high.

Within minutes of arriving on the scene, Derek dropped his gun belt, removed his shoes and headed to the river. A local resident who was assisting warned

Derek that it was deep, but it was too late. Derek took two steps in and quickly found himself pulled under. He came up sputtering, grabbed a branch, and, for a split second, thought about turning back. But he didn't.

Derek had a split-second decision to make. Fueled by thoughts of his seven-year-old son at home, he thought, "If I get swept away, in the unlikely event I survive, I will know I did everything I could to try to save the girl. If it were my child, I hope that someone would be willing to take the chance and save him." He wasn't scared. He decided to go.

Derek was able to reach the opposite side of the fallen tree to which Amy clung, but couldn't make it to her side because of his size and the other branches in the way. The terror in Amy's eyes was more frightening than the force of the river. The only way he could get to her was to break off the smaller branches growing out of the bigger one. He got to work.

While he was using all his physical strength to make his way to her, he talked to her, reassuring her that everything was going to be okay. He kept asking her if she could hold on just a little longer so he could get to her. With large, fearful eyes, she said she could.

Soon, Derek was able to reach her. He grabbed Amy around her waist and told her he was going to have to pull her under the water, under the branch. She agreed. He knew that one slight misstep could cost one or both of them their lives. These are the moments that police wish never happened.

Human life is precious; the life of a child even more so. Knowing that your grasp is the only thing that separates a child from life and death is a heavy burden. Although it may take a split second, those times feel like hours when you are praying that you are making the right choice. Should I wait for more help? Can she hang on long enough? What if the river pulls her from me? What if she can't hold her breath long enough? What if she panics and tries to break free?

These types of questions and fears run through a person's mind when they are trying to save someone. For a police officer, the decision has an even greater impact. He will be judged. If he can't hold on, if she can't hold her breath or the river takes her, he will be judged. He will be stupid for not waiting, he will be weak for not holding on tight enough, and he will be prosecuted in the court of public opinion without being able to defend himself. His picture will be displayed on the news alongside the image of the dead, innocent child.

You have seconds to decide. What will it be? Will you risk your life, your reputation, and your future to save this child or do you wait?

If you wait and she is lost, you still lose. This is the riddle of law enforcement: finding a way to do the right thing and succeeding at it, without upsetting or injuring anyone.

While Derek and the onlookers were praying Amy could hold her breath and Derek would succeed, someone else was notifying the parents that their child was trapped in the river. They were only a few miles away and they reached the scene quickly.

They were too late. When they arrived, Amy was already safe. Derek hadn't lost his grip and she held her breath long enough without panicking. When Derek signaled to the help on shore that Amy was safely with him, the on-shore officer was able to throw the flotation device out to them. Derek sandwiched Amy between himself and the device. The combination of the two men on shore pulling and Derek kicking and paddling with his free arm was enough to get them to shore safely.

The parents were greeted by a burly officer, who was soaking wet, taking notes and asking questions. Their nine-year-old daughter was safe on dry ground. Volunteer fire department members had also arrived and were checking everyone to make sure there were no injuries.

Despite the terror Amy had so recently experienced she was resilient, ready to go home and put on dry clothes. Just another day in the life of a kid. And a cop. Derek had to dry off and get back to work. Keep moving, that's what they do, from one crisis to another. Not all of them are this intense, but added together the crises can easily pile up and make your day feel like you have been pulled from a river.

It's been a year since Derek was hailed a hero for saving a life. Since then his wife says, "Be careful, I love you," a little more frequently. She understands what he does, but she worries about him. Worries that one day it will be him who is pulled down the river and she and their son will be standing on the shore trying to understand their grief.

It's still business as usual in his town. For Derek that means stopping to talk to people throughout the day, pushing kids on the swings in the park, and trying to let people know that he is there because he cares. It's this type of community policing that brought Derek to the job and keeps him there. He hopes his efforts aren't in vain and inspire others to be a little bit kinder in their own day-to-day lives. He also hopes that his reputation will precede him if an incident ever goes south. He hopes that people will remember he cares and that not all police interactions can have such happy endings.

Fred Stoldt
Married
3 Children, 2 Dogs
Active Since 1992
Ohio Police Officer
Favorite Ice Cream – Mint Chocolate Chip

CHAPTER TEN

FRED

Being a patrolman for 30 years was a conscious choice. I loved the streets, and unless I was injured you could find me there. I have saved children, been in numerous car chases, caught bank robbers, put murderers on death row, and participated in countless deeds that have amounted to just another day at the office. I was also a K-9 handler.

About 12 years ago, I had one of my most memorable moments. We were conducting some of our defensive driving training at our local shopping mall. We took turns racing our patrol vehicles through a number of traffic cones, strategically placed by instructors who haven't realized roads are wider than that.

I noticed a small pickup truck on the far side of the lot watching us. I took a drive over to the truck to discover a nine-year-old boy and his father. A father I had met before. Ignoring what I knew, I asked the boy if he'd like to take a ride and he shook his head with a fearful look. A few seconds later he whispered to his dad, who told me his boy changed his mind.

I closed my interior gate so my K-9 partner wouldn't scare the child. We buckled up and pulled up to the starting point. The Captain looked at my newly-acquired passenger then at me and said, "I trust you – don't make me regret it."

After the "get set, go," I hit the siren and lights and we moved quickly through the driving course. My K-9 began running in circles with excitement, and my passenger giggled with a glee I had never heard before. You'd swear he was being tickled relentlessly by invisible hands. When we finished the route, his face red with excitement, I drove towards his father's truck and asked if he had ever been in a police car. To my surprise, he replied, "No, but my daddy has." I laughed and returned him to his father. With a nod of understanding, we went our separate ways. I was comforted by the knowledge that he was willing to let his son trust me and judge based on his own experiences, not his father's. I assume that the father was feeling something similar, that I would treat his child with respect and kindness regardless of what I knew about him. It's those uneasy alliances we rely upon in the street.

I have always held the belief that this young man would never forget this encounter. I know I sure haven't.

Glenn K
Married
4 Children, 3 Cats
Sworn In 1970
Retired Connecticut Sergeant
Favorite Ice Cream – Chocolate & Peanut Butter

CHAPTER ELEVEN

GLENN

Glenn can't remember a time when he didn't want to be a police officer. There was no special incident that prompted him, it was just something he wanted to do. Immediately after high school, he took the test with the state and local police departments, and took the first position that became available; his thirteen-year career with his local police department began.

Despite the fact that he left the job after thirteen years to spend the next 23 as a prosecutor, you can tell that law enforcement is Glenn's first love. He still dreams that he is back in his uniform patrolling the street. Some men are lifetime cops; Glenn is one of them. He misses being on the streets and helping people.

Glenn's experiences ran the gamut, he worked undercover, which was like "play acting and getting paid." He worked in the Traffic Division which was "fabulous" because he was paid to ride a Harley. When he left to further his education, he had already become the youngest Sergeant in his department. All in all, it was a good career.

But it wasn't always good for his personal life. Being a law enforcement officer is difficult on the home front;

it's dangerous, the hours are long, the pay isn't great and the emotional toll is tremendous. Glenn's first marriage ended in divorce after nine years, which included a year undercover, requiring him to spend long nights in bars. It was more than the marriage could take. It didn't help that Glenn, like many officers, had a difficult time expressing himself. Rather than let himself experience his emotions, Glenn kept it bottled up inside. His frustration, fear, and anger wasn't something he and his wife were equipped to handle as a couple. He had a better time with his second wife; they have been married for 34 years.

Glenn spent a year in the 1970s trying to buy guns and drugs on the street in an effort to quell the violence of local motorcycle clubs. It's no surprise that people often ask him to "tell me a story". Glenn has lots of stories to tell, horrible suicides, car wrecks, catching burglars in the act and one that still upsets him to this day.

Every officer has that story. The victim whose name you will never forget. You remember everything from that day, what you were wearing, what they were wearing, the weather, the time of day, everything. In Glenn's neighborhood, there was a center where developmentally-challenged children and young adults could work. It was a great opportunity for them to use their talents. There was a twenty-five-year-old man who would ride his bike back and forth each day. One day, a bus was approaching and he panicked, falling off his bike. His head was crushed by the bus.

Glenn will never forget standing there with this young man's body and an incredible feeling of helplessness. A crowd was gathering; he could hear onlookers gasping in disbelief, others sobbing. He could offer no hope for the young man or the crowd. The gruesome scene, coupled with the fact that there was absolutely nothing he could do to help this man or his family, weighed heavily on him. He knew that the unsuspecting parents would most likely crumble in each other's arms when the officers arrived on their doorstep to deliver the news. There was no sliver of hope, no chance to say goodbye, not even the ability to look him in the face to identify their beloved child. All Glenn could do was secure the scene and wait until he was alone to cry.

Glenn doesn't tell that story often, he doesn't like to. The emotions are overwhelming and he knows there are plenty of sad stories to go around. He'd much rather tell you the story of the handsome, young officer that replied to the call of a barking dog.

One Saturday afternoon, while Glenn was patrolling a small Connecticut city, he received a call of a barking dog continuously near a wooded area. "When I arrived, I could hear the distressed barking. I parked my bike and went to investigate. This would prove to be trickier than it looked.

"The area was very densely wooded and it took me nearly an hour to get to the source of the barking. The entire time, I was sweating through my uniform and getting scratches from the underbrush. If it weren't for my tall leather boots, I surely would have ripped my pants.

"When I reached the source, I found a small dog attached to a leash which had become entangled in the woods. I radioed headquarters and told them what I had. Dispatch found a notice for a missing dog; the owners had been looking for him for five days. While I freed the little guy and started the long trek back to the road, they called the family to let them know what I had found.

"With Fido in one arm, I began the journey back to the street. This was more difficult than going in. I didn't want the dog to receive any injuries from the brush.

When I finally broke free, the family was there. They all (mom, dad, two kids) ran up and hugged both me and their dog.

"Hot, sweaty, scratched, and dressed in a now filthy uniform, it was one of the most rewarding little experiences in my career."

Glenn likes this story because it is light-hearted with a happy ending. Much of police work falls into another category. He also likes to tell it because people expect to hear stories of heartbreak and violence. He likes to remind them there is much more to police work. More than they hear and see on the news.

And the stories that don't make the news are often the most important of all.

Alison
Single
2 Children, 3 Dogs
Active Since 1992
Massachusetts Detective
Favorite Ice Cream – Mint Chocolate Chip

CHAPTER TWELVE

ALISON

Alison is a detective assigned primarily to sex crimes. There aren't a lot of feel-good stories coming out of those assignments. Now that she has her chance in the public spotlight, she is making the most of it and hoping to raise awareness to prevent animal cruelty.

Even though her father was a police officer for 30 years, she wasn't prepared for the things she would see on the job: the anger, pain, frustration and sadness of society. Responding to calls where you will find a child crying, a wife beaten, or worse, can cause you to wonder where the good is. What causes you to take out your frustrations on another human being?

On February 6, 2014, Alison wondered what would cause a person to take out his frustration on a helpless puppy. Officer Brian Shameklis responded to a call of potential animal abuse. When he arrived at the scene and saw the blood on the side of the residents' pick-up truck, he knew it was more than an allegation. When an officer sees blood at a scene, they need to prepare themselves for the worst. They don't know if what they find will give them nightmares in the days to come.

After determining that a four-month-old Pomeranian had been beaten with pruning shears and left for dead in a snow bank, Officer Shameklis, Alison, two other officers and a dispatcher were determined to find the puppy. When the suspect brought the officers to the general area where the pup had been dumped, they began searching the area with flashlights. With no sounds of despair or pain greeting them, they feared the dog was dead. They soon found a black and red mass in the snow, barely moving but hanging on to life. Because there was so much blood, they had no idea what kind of injuries the dog had. Their hearts sank at the sight.

Once again, they were called to a situation that would bring them to the point of tears; they were called upon to make right of a situation that no one should have to see. It was in that moment that Alison felt anger, horror, and anguish. How could someone do this to an eight-pound puppy? What kind of person is so careless with a helpless being? What did this dog do to deserve this horrific beating? He pooped in his crate. A perfectly predictable action by a young dog set off a series of events that would show the deep compassion and generosity of a police department and the community it serves.

Alison's son left a sweatshirt in the back of her car. They were able to wrap the puppy in the soft, worn cotton for warmth. While Alison drove, another officer held the pup in his lap; all the bleeding animal could do was stare at them, his big brown eyes full of terror and pleading. None of them knew what the fate of the dog, named Scrunchy, would be.

When they arrived at the Boston Road Animal Hospital, the veterinarian and staff worked to evaluate the little puppy. They determined that Scrunchy was in grave condition and would need brain surgery. His medical bills would near $10,000. The dog's owner and her boyfriend, the offender, had no money to repair the damage done.

Imagine you are standing in a field holding something so fragile that if you move the wrong way, it will shatter. You are all alone and you can see people in the background, but they can't, or won't help you, they are expecting you to choose the right path. That's how Alison felt at that moment. She was holding the fragile life of another being in her hand. She needed to make a decision that would determine its fate.

Many people might have decided that it was in Scrunchy's best interest, and a wiser use of funds, to humanely euthanize him. Alison's heart was already too far gone; she needed this pup to survive so that she knew her job wasn't always in vain. It would be a ray of sunshine for her.

Alison took out her credit card and told them to proceed. She would pay the initial costs and find a way to get the money for Scrunchy's care. She also decided that if this dog were going to have a new start, he'd need a new name. Thus was born Jameson Jamie James.

Getting the funds needed to pay for Jameson's surgery wouldn't be easy. Where was an officer with two kids going to find $10,000? A K-9 officer at her station reached out to his friends; they reached out to theirs and before she knew it the media had gotten hold of the story and people began offering to help.

What was most touching to Alison was that the public called the station and asked where to send money. Alison never asked, they simply offered. Children and animals hit our hearts harder than anything else; the desire to make a bad situation better for them becomes a passionate crusade. That's exactly what happened for Jameson. Because of the generosity of strangers, Jameson received all the treatment he needed and was adopted by Alison and her family.

The outpouring of support and concern was overwhelming, "For us to come to work and to save the dog first of all," Alison said, "and then to have the whole animal-lover community band together to try to save one dog — it's refreshing and it's heartwarming — and we don't see that every day." Hundreds of people attended a vigil after Jameson left the hospital so all of his well-wishers could see the amazing little dog that stole the hearts of an entire police department. A dog that should fear people but has learned to trust, love and entertain those he encounters.

The excitement in Alison's voice is still palpable; she has created a greater bond with her community, saved a life, and found a new mission. Jameson has his own Facebook page, "Jameson's Journey," which features some pretty funny videos of Jameson at home with his new sisters, trouble-making Dalmatian Delilah and the cool-headed Golden Retriever, Tilly. My personal favorite is when Jameson turns himself into a "reverse Dalmatian." Alison turned a tragedy into a story that everyone can continue to follow; Jameson posts updates about animals in need as well as anecdotes from his new life.

The Facebook page is only a start for Alison. She wants Jameson to become an ambassador against animal cruelty and to get the message out to the world that it's not okay to hurt animals, ever. Measures to prevent animal cruelty are starting to make their way to the House and Senate, and bills are being passed in many states which will hold people accountable for their actions when they harm animals. Alison wants people to help make that happen. She holds fundraisers for local shelters and, with the help of Jameson, is keeping the issue in the public eye. She, like many officers, is using her power for good.

CHAPTER THIRTEEN

BETWEEN A MOTHER AND CHILD

Age 4
"Bye Daddy! Don't get dead."

"Oh honey, why would you say that to Daddy?"

"Because, I don't want the bad guys to kill him to-night."

"No one is going to hurt him; he has other officers to help."

"Then why is he always alone?"

I don't know.

"Because they like to have the police in different cars, that way if his breaks down, his help is in a car that works fine."

Age 6
"Why can't Daddy be home for Christmas dinner? Don't the bad guys know it's a holiday?"

I don't know.

"Of course they do, but police should be out there just in case someone gets in an accident."

Age 7

"Why doesn't Daddy like me to tell people he is a police officer?"

You're too young to understand.

"Well, even though most people like police, there are some people who don't like them. Daddy just likes to keep it a secret."

Age 8

"Why can't Dad come to my game tonight?"

I don't want to have to tell you.

"Well, sometimes the parents on the opposite team have done something bad and it's easier if Dad just doesn't go. But he'll be at tomorrow's game, don't worry!"

Age 9

"Why did one of my friends say that police are bad and all they do is beat people up?"

I don't know.

"Oh honey, not everyone likes the police and sometimes they say things that aren't true. You know your Dad isn't bad and doesn't beat people up, right?"

"Yes, but they didn't believe me."

Ageless

"Mom, why did those police officers get shot?"

I don't know.

"Mom, why is everyone mad at the police?"

I don't know.

"Is someone going to kill Dad someday?"

I don't know

I don't know

I don't know........

Sid H.
Widower
2 Children, 1 Cat, 2 Dogs
Active Since 2001
California Police Officer
Favorite Ice Cream – Moose Tracks

CHAPTER -FOURTEEN

SID

Note: All italicized text in this section comes from posts Jessie made to an online support group, Police-Wives.org. Although we've never met in person, we've spoken on the phone and she was the kind of friend who really cared.

There's always that Facebook friend whose feed you will either love or hate, and, for me, Jessie was that friend. Although I did enjoy her photos mocking the local weatherman's choice of ties, I wanted to reach through the computer and break her keyboard when she posted about politics or social issues. We weren't always on the same page. Unfortunately, I no longer have to steel myself for her posts and wonder if I am going to be amused or annoyed when I log in. Jessie passed away on September 30, 2014 of a terminal illness. She's not in this book because she's a police officer; she is in this book because she is Sid's wife and Sid is a police officer. To understand Sid's story, you've got to understand Jessie's.

It often feels like we always speak well of the dead, but believe me when I say I am not speaking well of Jessie because she is not here. I am speaking well of her because she was one of those people who was a friend to everyone and possessed a bigger heart than anyone I have ever met. She was the kind of person who called you, no matter what kind of pain she was in, even if she thought you had a hang nail. Really.

It's no wonder Sid was smitten with Jessie and would find in her the woman with whom he wanted to spend the rest of his life. They first met on Sid's 21st birthday; oddly enough, he bought his first gun from her. They were both married at the time and it was a chance meeting, two people making small talk and going their separate ways. Little did they know that they would become such integral parts of each other's lives.

A few years later, Sid was divorced from his first wife and was bowling with Jessie's brother and sister, when he noticed a cute new girl at the register. Jessie's sister, Kathy, made sure Sid knew who Jessie was. Sid didn't need much prodding. Jessie was attractive, smart and had a beautiful laugh. Since she was working the register, Sid needed more change that evening than a baby's diaper.

"As I passed the front counter one of those times, Jessie said, 'I thought you were married.' I said, 'I was.' She said 'me too.' We looked at each other and smiled as I went back to my lane," Sid said.

"I thought about that for the next few weeks. I bowled twice each week, always coming up with more reasons to go talk to Jessie.

"One evening, my friend Jim told me I should get Jessie's number. I told him I planned to. So, Jim decided to go to the front desk and ask Jessie what chance I would have of getting her number if I asked her. Apparently her answer was 'Better than most. And they're slim to none.' I imagine Jim zipping away like Witch Hazel from Looney Tunes, leaving bobby pins tumbling in the air.

"Jim came to me as I was tying my street shoes and said, 'Dude, you better go get her number.' I looked over and saw Jessie counting her drawer down so I didn't want to bother her. I said I would talk to her when she wasn't busy. Jim said, 'no dude, you need to get her number now.' When I looked back, Jessie was walking toward the door with her purse slung over her shoulder and her hair flowing behind her.

"I stood up and started walking beside her and we talked our way to the parking lot. We talked for about an hour, and then exchanged phone numbers. She always liked to comment on the fact that I gave her three phone numbers.

"I called her the next day and invited her to dinner. She asked if she could bring her eight-month-old, because they were a package deal. If I wanted to date her, I'd be dating her kid too. I said I was good with that. The three of us went to dinner and the rest is history.

"I broke several personal rules to date Jessie. I always said I wouldn't date a woman who was older than me, a woman with a kid, a woman who was divorced, or a woman who smoked. I was able to get her to quit smoking. As for the rest of the rules? Well, rules are made to be broken right?

"She was worth it."

Their relationship took its course. Jessie and Sid married in 2001. They both had dreams – Sid's was to become a police officer, Jessie's was to become a licensed Pharmacy Technician. Armed with a plan and a lot of patience, they made all their dreams come true, including their dream to build a house.

Sid was up first. He became a reserve police officer, then worked weekends and went to school full time for a year to meet the requirements for the academy. "When I was in school and when I went through the academy in

2005 it was incredibly valuable to have Jessie able to care for the apartment (at the time), and the boys without my direct assistance," he said. "I was able to do my homework without having to worry about anything. She was amazing."

Sid had two uncles in the California Highway Patrol. One of his earliest memories was of Uncle CW coming by while on duty. Sid loved to hear his uncle's duty belt creaking whenever he moved. "I don't recall a time when I didn't want to be a police officer," he said. "My grandma used to say I said since I was five years old that I wanted to be a cop. My uncles would occasionally show up with their patrol cars and uniforms and I always knew that had to be me someday. It's a calling, I guess. Jessie often said I was meant to be a cop because I'm honest almost to a fault, my integrity is infallible, and I genuinely care about the plight of others."

Once Sid was settled into his position, Jessie was able to pursue her dream. In January 2010, she got her license.

"The state FINALLY processed my Pharmacy Technician application! As of this morning, I am officially a Pharmacy Technician licensed by California!!! I can find a job now!! This started back in December 2008, and is completed now!! OMG, I am SO happy, I can't tell you. WOOHOOO!!!!!!!!!!!!!!!!!!!"

With their careers settled, two kids and two full-time jobs, Sid and Jessie decided to build a house. Everything was falling into place.

Then everything fell out of place.

Jessie was diagnosed with cancer in 2011. It was diagnosed as breast cancer because that is where it began, but by July 2011 it was in her lymph node, breast and bones. She began chemotherapy. Sid took a few days off to be with her. He was there when she received the news that she had cancer and he wanted to be there when she got any news, good or bad. CT scans, MRIs and PET scans would become all too familiar to both of them.

December brought them good news - *The cancer is just about all gone. What little is left is going to be treated with radiation and oral meds. I'm winning! There was hardly anything left to see. I need to see the endocrinologist for my thyroid issues, but I can live with that.*

Six months later, things still looked good. The cancer that remained in Jessie's body wasn't growing, but she was still ill from all the treatments she had received and couldn't sit or stand for the eight hours that was required at her job. With a heavy heart, she resigned.

"I told her we could make it on my income, however difficult it would be," Sid said. "She just couldn't do it anymore and she felt rotten about it for the rest of her life. I never let her feel too bad, because I always wanted her to know I absolutely didn't hold it against her. The thing she said that always bugged me was 'I'm sorry this is happening.' I had to convince her that it was not her fault that she got cancer. She did nothing to deserve it, or earn it. It was a shitty situation all around, but it was not her fault her boobs were trying to kill her. She would laugh, but she still always felt guilty. It broke my heart.

"It wasn't the hospital bills that were the problem. It was the fact that she had to stop working and the bills piled up in general. We had to run credit cards up to survive and I'm still trying to figure out how to deal with that. Medical costs were never more than $1000 in any given year. It was survival expenses and still is.

"When she was working, we managed. When she stopped working, I put on the best face I could for her. We could afford the house with both of us working. I've had to find ways to cut other corners with only one income."

Finances weren't the only thing Sid had to worry about; he had two boys who were losing their mother. How do you prepare a child for his mother's death? How was Sid to help the boys watch their mother slip away little by little while his heart was slipping away with her? Sid and Jessie had a love that was enviable, they always slept with a least one part of their bodies touching and they finished each other's sentences. The void that was about to be created could never, ever be closed. Not for Sid, not for Jessie's sons.

Now you know a little about Sid and Jessie, you can see how they worked as a team to fulfill their dreams only to see them shaken by cancer. What does this have to do with Sid being a cop? Everything I want you to know. Sid is not just a cop, he is a human being. He has a life. He doesn't just magically appear in a blue uniform and a badge at the start of his shift. He is just like everyone else. He has bills, a family, heartache and joy. Just like every single person out there – criminals and good citizens alike.

Most people get up and go to a work, grab some coffee, talk to the people in the cubicles next to them, and some even goof off while they are at work. The career of a police officer isn't as easy. They are often alone, when they take a coffee break the public sees them as wasting taxpayers' money and when they stop someone for breaking the law the first question they are asked isn't usually "How are you doing today, officer?" Even if it were, they wouldn't tell you. That's not how it works; there's not a lot of social interaction in their typical stop.

Sid was lucky. He worked the day shift, which helped. He could be with Jessie and the boys nights. Other officers might not be so lucky since nights, weekends and holidays need to be covered. Crime doesn't stop for anyone.

"Cancer didn't change anything about how I dealt with members of the public in general, but a few times I have had drivers use cancer (their own or that of a family member) as an excuse for their poor driving," Sid said. "I generally have explained to them that my wife managed to obey traffic laws despite her disease, as I pointed to the pink ribbon pin on the pocket flap of my uniform shirt.

"I found I was beginning to get a bit bitter toward people with bad attitudes, and I had a little difficulty holding my tongue sometimes. I caught myself making a few off-hand comments I would not have normally made, and I became less adept at hiding 'how I really feel' when dealing with the typical mouthy asshole. Nothing that would get me in trouble, but less than my normal professional self.

"I started to become really bitter about a lot of things, but never toward Jessie. I found that I was less tolerant of the standard bullshit I got from people I came into contact with during the day. I'd snap off a smart-assed remark at them and was starting to feel like I was being very unprofessional. I didn't like that, and I had to work hard to avoid doing it.

"People's excuses suddenly started sounding really trite to me. It wasn't as if their issues were any less significant than mine. It was more that even with what Jessie and I were going through, we still managed to do the right thing and take responsibility for our own mistakes. I will be the first to admit it when I screw up, and I guess I just expect that from everyone. Nothing changed about the way people responded to being stopped. What changed was how I responded to their excuses."

Typical cop, right? Not caring about anyone but themselves. Not quite. Sid is like the hundreds of thousands of good cops out there. He held his tongue; he let people make remarks not knowing the impact they were having on him. After all, cops aren't supposed to have feelings. Sid was simply doing his job, and too often people forget that their reaction to him can set the tone. They have no idea what is going through an officer's head; they simply see the inconvenience to themselves. Meanwhile, as Sid stated, officers are doing their best to hold their tongues and not react to the way people treat them.

So why didn't he choose a different career path if this was so challenging? Ha! Caught you! You are only seeing the negative. Perhaps Sid loves his job; perhaps it's not so hard when there is cooperation and support. There is a lot of good in police work, but it has to come from both sides. Let's rephrase the question: did he think about leaving the force once Jessie was diagnosed?

Despite the stress and difficulties, Sid never thought about changing careers, even after Jessie was diagnosed. "Absolutely not," he said. "My career choice was almost preordained, to hear my grandmother tell it. In fact, I am so thankful to have the job I have, in the city where I work.

"Once Jessie was diagnosed, I was pretty numb for a while. I was off work for a few weeks to support her physically and emotionally as she went to all of the preliminary appointments to prepare her plan of treatment.

"Once I returned to work, I didn't really feel any different, but I began to notice that I was thinking of her constantly when I had nothing specific to do. I would think about what was happening to her, what treatments were going to work and how they'd affect her, not knowing how long she was to be with me, what would I do when she was gone, what would the results of the next PET scan hold.

"Other times we got reports that the cancer had progressed, sometimes a little, and sometimes a lot. That was when my brain really kicked into overdrive. 'What are we going to do now? Why aren't the researchers coming up with a cure? Is there even a cure possible? I hate that she's in pain.'

"It is not easy to make me feel powerless, but cancer did that. I am supposed to be able to protect her. She called me her Knight in Shiny Armor, but what kind of knight am I if I can't save her from this?

"We are a local police department of forty-five sworn. We are small enough that everybody knows everybody. My coworkers have always liked Jessie, and they always asked how she's doing. When they heard she was coming home into hospice, they kicked into support mode. They started coming to the house to cook for us, did our laundry, and paid for housekeepers to clean the house and sanitize it for Jessie. Since Jessie passed, they have continued to bring food because they know I don't cook, and they regularly check on us to see if there is anything we need.

"After Jessie passed, my Chief called me to personally express her condolences. Where else is the Chief of Police going to call you personally? I could not dream of having any other career, or for that matter, even working for a different department. I am exactly where I belong."

As for defining moments on the job, Sid hit it square on the head and I couldn't help but laugh. "A law enforcement career is a string of defining moments with a lot of boredom in between."

Sid was awarded Officer of the Year in 2013. He was unanimously nominated by the sergeants, and the Chief didn't bat an eye when she heard his name. Sid was willing to go to work at a moment's notice to process a crime scene or handle a major crash. He knew that he couldn't have done it without Jessie.

"Any time the phone would ring and I'd get that look on my face, she just said, 'Go. I got this.' Even with chemo, pain and unruly boys, I knew she could handle herself until I got back home," Sid said. "She never gave me any grief about leaving for things like that. She almost made it easy.

"I focused my (Officer of the Year) speech on her, and when I started talking directly to her from the podium, nobody was looking at me anymore. Their attention was right where it needed to be. Squarely on Jessie. That award was hers as much as it was mine. She was proud of all of my career accomplishments, but she was really proud of Officer of the Year."

Unfortunately, around the same time Sid and Jessie got the news that her cancer was back.

"Well, the cancer is back and growing in my spine again. I'm in more pain, and not sure what treatment I'm going to be starting when we come back from our trip. My oncologist said we're going to test my hormone levels, and depending on if I'm pre or really post-menopausal it'll vary. I'm either going to try some hormonal treatment, even though I was on tamoxifen and that didn't work. Or I'm going onto a different infused chemo and it may be one drug or a combo of two drugs. If it's the two-drug combo, I'm going to have my bloodwork very closely monitored because the treatment destroys red and white blood cells as well as platelets. On the up side, it's not supposed to make my hair fall out. No word yet on if this is the last thing we have to throw at it or not. Thanks for being with me through all this."

"I found out I've already beaten the odds by making it past two years. Two years!! Can you believe that shit? That two years is a significant milestone? I'm going to make it to five years, and then I'll set my mark for ten, dammit!!"

I never got to ask her if I could put her and Sid in this book; I always thought she had more time. I thought I could ask her in October once she was feeling better and I had gotten through the rest of the interviews. I didn't get that chance.

In June of 2014, Jessie posted this update on PW.

"I've been feeling very guilty about not getting on here in ages. I know I "see" a lot of you on FB, but I met you here and I feel bad. If you know me, then you know what's been going on the last 3 years. Well, the cancer is growing in a lymph node behind my left collarbone. I'm so mad I could scream. I've been on chemo for over a year, A YEAR, and the bastard is growing! My oncologist says it's small and we'll keep an eye on it, and if it starts to get bad (like it growing isn't bad), we'll change chemo. I've been walking around either numb, angry, or shaken.

Today Sid asked if I was ok. When I said no and that this latest development had me down, he asked what he could do to make me feel better. I wish he could make it go away. I wish he could make US go away for a while. I wish I didn't feel so damn helpless. I've been able to keep it together for a while now, but I'm tired. I'm tired of hurting, tired of being sick after chemo, tired of putting a positive face on this for everyone. I don't want pity, I just want a break from it all..."

Despite all of that, Jessie was on PW in late July responding to someone who was concerned about an upcoming biopsy. *"Hi, I'm Jessie, and I've been fighting cancer for three years now. Waiting for the biopsy re-*

sults is the worst. You're on eggshells, and trying not to think about it. Are you on Facebook? If you are and want to send me a friend request, just remind me you're from PW. You can also send me a PM when you see me here. I'll be praying for you."

This is why Sid loved her so much. Jessie could kill you with kindness.

So what's next for Sid?

"I hope my mind will be clearer when I do return to work," he said. "I don't have to think about her cancer or its ultimate outcome anymore, and there's no more 'not knowing' on that front. Now the question that keeps rolling over and over in my head is 'what does the future hold for the boys and me?'

"I truly don't know the answer to that. I do know we will carry on. I know we will always have her memory, her pictures, and little things to always remind us of her (like the box of Tic Tacs she always had in the center console in her car). I know I will never forget her and never stop loving her. But I also know life is very lonely without her here, and I don't do well with lonely. I still wear my wedding ring, and I don't want to take it off. I still feel married, but she's not here anymore. It's a conundrum I'm going to have to sort out at some point during this whole 'moving forward' thing.

"For now, I continue as if she is still here. I still look at her picture when I eat my veggies at dinnertime; because it's her fault I'm eating them at all. I still tell the boys to do the things Jessie always told them to do. I even half-jokingly say 'If I don't make you do it, your mom will haunt me for it.'

"I suppose that is one thing that fits into the 'seeing things differently' category. Cancer was always something you heard about on television and something that happened to someone else. We never really talked about it. Then after her diagnosis, it became an unavoidable part of our life. We worked through the initial shock, sadness and anger, and we learned to live with it, and with the fact that it could take her someday.

"We got to the point that we could even joke about cancer. Gallows humor, for sure. We'd walk past someone smoking, and we'd gag and cough, and one of us would say 'Don't breathe that shit. It'll give you cancer.' Her disease became part of our life, but cancer did not control our life or our lives. Yes, there is a difference. Our life is the life we built together, while our lives are what we live individually, if that makes any kind of sense.

"I began to react differently when I'd hear the word cancer from others. When a co-worker's mother died of cancer, it hit me hard even though I never knew her. I began to really notice the large number of commercials and magazine ads centered on cancer prevention, cancer awareness and cancer treatments.

"Now that Jessie is gone, I really hate the commercials that show cancer survivors and tell the stories of how they beat cancer and they're still here to tell about it. I have to control my animosity toward these people, because my Jessie is NOT here to tell her story anymore. She certainly got an extra two years of good quality life because of the chemotherapy drugs, but that doesn't change the fact that she is gone now. I do not begrudge these people for their survival. I applaud them for it. But I don't want to hear about it anymore.

"As I write this, my Jessie has been gone for two weeks today. It is still fresh, but it seems like an eternity has passed. The wounds are healing, however slowly. I still cry every day, and I still think about her every minute of every day. I still have little triggers that set me off. Seeing an unexpected picture of her, seeing her toothbrush on the counter, watching a video on YouTube that I forgot she was in. I lose it and sob for a few minutes. Maybe it's not very manly of me, and I'm supposed to be the tough, gruff cop, but I don't really give a tinker's damn what other people think of me right now. The people who are important to me understand, because they also cry for Jessie and her dad every day.

"One of the boys said the other day that he was ready to get back to school so he'd feel normal. I had to explain that normal is gone. We will have to build a new normal. We have to move forward with our lives. We will never forget Jessie. She truly is unforgettable.

"I am thankful she is not in pain anymore, and I'm glad in some way that her dad did not have to be here to go on without his baby. He passed a week and a half before her, so she outlived both her parents. The world is an emptier place without them.

"Finally, I'd say watching the love of my life, my other half, the person I was supposed to spend forever with.... watching the life drain from her body while she looked into my eyes, was far and away the most difficult thing I have ever done in my life. But knowing she went peacefully and in relative comfort, and that I was the last thing she saw in this life makes it just a little more bearable. It would be unfair to have her die in a hospital while I was somewhere else. I owed her that much.

"Life will never be the same for those who are left. We have to realign our goals and desires to account for the missing. That's what I call Jessie, her dad and her mom. They are the missing, because they are physically gone from our lives, and there is a huge void each of them used to occupy.

"I cannot replace Jessie. Nor would I ever try. She is irreplaceable. There will always be emptiness in my chest when I see a picture of her. I will not ever again allow myself to become bitter about her disease or her death. To do so would be a dishonor to her memory.

"I never dishonored her in life, and I could never dishonor her in death.

"We will go on. We will move forward. We will always remember. We will honor her life and her memory."

Damien
Single
Active Since 2013
North Dakota Police Officer
Favorite Ice Cream – Cookies and Cream

CHAPTER FIFTEEN

DAMIEN

Listening to Damien, you can't help but smile. At age 25, he's not yet jaded by what he's seen. In just under two years on the job, he's witnessed child abuse and death. "Death, especially the suicide, makes you step back and realize how much we take for granted," he said. "How short life is. Some of the things people do really blows your mind. Some things don't make any sense." He believes that by taking a step back and seeing it through their eyes, it's easier to manage in your own head. The ghosts might not haunt you as long.

After receiving a degree in criminal justice, Damien knew that he wanted a career in law enforcement. He fell in love with the fact that police wear many hats and every day is different. "One day you're a plumber, then a counselor and then you are out directing traffic." He gets to see a little bit of everything, and everyone. His love for the profession grows daily, no matter what he sees. However, some of the things affect him more deeply than others.

One evening, a local grocery store clerk called 9-1-1 to report a shoplifting in progress. By the time Damien arrived, the suspect had already fled but the employees at the store knew the name of the subject as he was a former employee. When Damien arrived at his house, an apartment in a low-income housing development, he was outside and had already dumped the bacon he stole for fear of being caught with it. Rather than arrest him, Damien let the suspect go with a promise to appear at his court date.

Although this put the suspect at ease, Damien felt compelled to do more. He asked the young man why he stole the bacon. He didn't expect the reply he received. The young man broke down in tears and explained that he lives with his young nephew, cousin, aunt, and uncle. There's rarely enough food for everyone. He just wanted to make his nephew his favorite dish, a dish that they haven't had in a long time because they couldn't afford it.

Police work is a catch-22: you have a job to do but you also have to try to understand where people are coming from. What motivated them to commit this act? Damien had done his job; the suspect had been notified of his appearance in court and the grocery store was satisfied with the outcome. Now he wanted to do more. He asked the suspect what dish the nephew loved that was worth stealing for.

Armed with the list of ingredients, Damien headed to the store to pick up what was needed. When he returned to the residence, the expressions of happiness on the suspect's face and on that of his nephew were all Damien needed as payment. They were thankful, awed, and they cried. It was a surprise that they certainly didn't expect from a man sent to arrest a shoplifter. Damien knew these boys needed to believe the police weren't all bad. There were too many people in the area who didn't like the police. Damien didn't want this household to be among those people. He wants people to believe that police officers can be role models. His hope is that for every good deed performed, a crime will be averted.

For that reason, Damien participates in the Adopt-A-Cop program at the local elementary school. During his shift, he goes to the school to spend a little time with the kids there; he loves playing football with them. Starting his day making kids smile and feel safe makes him feel good. He knows that this interaction could change the way the children treat police in the future. There is a small window of opportunity in which he can shape their opinions. He's doing everything he can to make sure their experiences are positive.

Unfortunately, not every encounter can be good. "Sometimes subjects just cuss you out," Damien said. "Then I wonder why I am trying to help when they clearly don't want me to. But then I go to the next subject and they are grateful for my help." He's just doing the best he can in a complicated profession.

Even though he's been on the job a short time, he sees the complexity of his situation and he is frustrated by it. He is discouraged when he sees the news media jump to conclusions, and grouping all police officers into one bucket compounds his frustration. Damien articulated it pretty simply when he said, "If a teacher or fireman does something bad, people are mad at the one teacher or one fireman. They don't get mad at all teachers and firemen. They don't get grouped under the same umbrella. They are treated as individuals. When a police officer does something wrong, every cop becomes bad. No matter what we do, we aren't seen as individuals. We're just people doing the best we can to help other people."

Damien wants to stay in law enforcement for the rest of his life, but he already has some doubts. He's concerned about all the negativity and gun violence, and wonders if it's really worth it. Will it all have been in vain? A family with children is something he wants for his future, but he's not yet sure how it will fit with his career choice. Right now, he just wants to do his job and hope for the best. He loves his profession and hopes it will have more public support in the future.

Danny
Married
2 Dogs
Active Since 2007
Nevada Detective
Favorite Ice Cream – Cherry

CHAPTER SIXTEEN

DANNY

Although a gun is a mandatory piece of equipment, no officer wants to use it. An officer snaps his gun into his holster every day hoping that he doesn't have to take it out again until the shift is over and in truth, there are significantly more officers who have not fired their weapons than officers who have. Many never even draw their weapon for years.

Danny never expected to be in the minority. Danny patrols what is called a "zero tolerance" area: an area with a very high incidence of crime, most often violent. In a zero tolerance area, an officer can speak to and cite an individual who is breaking any law at all, including something as minor as jaywalking. Jaywalking is exactly what caused Danny, at age 28, to fire his gun one year into the job.

Danny and a nineteen-year-old cadet were on a routine patrol of a high-crime area. The morning had been uneventful thus far. There was the usual stop to grab coffee, talk to some of the neighbors about what was going on in the news and a text from his wife telling him to have a good day. Nothing to indicate that Danny would be a changed man by the end of the shift.

Danny spotted a man walking across the street dodging cars. As Danny went to speak to him, the man began to run. Running isn't a crime, but running away from a police officer for no apparent reason is suspicious, and a good cop will follow to find out why. Danny and the cadet followed in the cruiser until Danny had to get out of the car and continue the chase on foot. The cadet remained in the cruiser and called for assistance.

An officer learns many things in the academy. One of them is the importance of observation. While running, Danny observed the man and his clothing, jeans, a black t-shirt and a white undershirt. As the suspect ran, he began to pull up the outer t-shirt. For Danny, this was a red flag. Drug dealers in his patrol area were known to wear an outer shirt to cover the packets of drugs they had tucked into their pants. To avoid being caught, they pull up their shirts and toss out whatever drugs they are carrying.

This time there were no drugs. Instead, Danny saw a large-frame semi-automatic hand gun. As the suspect turned and aimed his gun at the cadet still seated in the vehicle, Danny reacted the way his training demanded.

He drew his weapon and fired two shots at the suspect. The suspect continued to try to evade, and Danny realized they were heading into an area he called a "fatal funnel". If Danny moved in any closer, they would be surrounded by buildings on three sides with little chance of escape. One of them would have to be shot or surrender for the other to escape.

To avoid this, Danny had to follow his suspect without closing himself off. As if reading Danny's mind, the man ran behind a tractor-trailer and climbed the wall behind it. On one side of the truck was an agitated person with a gun, on the other a police officer with a gun.

Inside the truck were innocent people, now caught in the cross fire.

Danny quickly assessed the situation to determine the best way to keep everyone safe. Before he could process much, the suspect flattened himself on the wall and took aim at Danny. Danny fired off two more rounds, and saw the man roll off the wall. Danny, believing he had hit the suspect in the head, broadcast a message to that effect over the radio.

All of the action happened in less than two minutes. Two minutes to run after someone, focus on what they are doing, check the surroundings for innocent bystanders, decide whether or not to shoot your weapon and try to keep up so that a person wielding a handgun does not get away. Two minutes.

As in most traumatic instances, time passes quickly and slowly. Quickly in that the actual time passed on the clock was quite short. Slowly for the participant, every moment seeming to take hours. Danny experienced that feeling for the first time that day. While he was running, his adrenaline was pumping and he heard nothing but his heart beating in his ears. He didn't hear the two shots fired at him. He saw the situation, kept his head and reacted in the best way he knew how. He drew on his training and his desire to not let a dangerous person, an armed suspect aiming a gun, and who could also injure innocent civilians, get away.

The occupants of the truck were shaken, but unharmed. They would later prove to be valuable, unbiased witnesses to the incident. Their account of the events would help to put Danny's mind at ease in the coming days, help ease the guilt he would feel over shooting at another human being. But that would come later.

When the back-up units arrived on the other side of the wall, instead of lying on the ground, the suspect was nowhere to be found. A man was on the loose with a gun, possibly injured, and not afraid to use it. Things became more frustrating and dangerous for everyone involved.

Danny was front and center in a situation where no officer wants to find himself. Panic set in: shots had been fired, Danny believed he had hit the man, no one was in custody, and one young man with a badge stood alone holding a smoking gun. It wouldn't be long before the story hit the media and people would start asking and accusing. Meanwhile, Danny's heart and head were racing.

Before Danny could deal with his feelings, there was a suspect to find. The K-9 unit was brought in and was unable to track his whereabouts. The recovery of three shell casings from the suspect's gun at the scene was an indication that he was dangerous and the police needed to find him before he used the gun again.

While the SWAT team was brought in, Danny and his cadet were sent to the FBI building for processing. Danny was relieved of his weapon. He and the cadet were put in separate rooms and were advised of their Garrity Rights, which protect public employees from being forced to incriminate themselves during interviews conducted by their employers.

Although the shooting occurred at noon, Danny didn't return home until almost midnight. He spent twelve hours trying to understand the events of that day. When he left that night, Danny still believed he had shot the suspect. He wouldn't know until the next day that he had missed.

Replaying the day's events over and over in his head, wondering if he could have done things differently,

Danny got little sleep. The belief he had shot someone weighed heavily on his mind, making him scared and nervous. He didn't know if he had killed someone, if he was going to be fired, go to jail or, perhaps most importantly, if he would ever forgive himself.

TV often portrays officer-involved shootings as casual events, with officers back on duty almost immediately. But the truth is different. After such an event, there is a comprehensive investigation. Aerial photos were taken, and Danny had to use colored markers to draw out the scene, account for all the bullets, and explain the situation multiple times, forcing him to relive and remember the events. The investigation after a shooting is painstakingly thorough. No officer wants to walk away with any doubt about what happened; right or wrong, they want the truth.

While Danny was documenting the incident, the SWAT team was conducting a "knock and talk," going door to door in the surrounding apartment buildings looking for signs of the suspect. It didn't take long before an elderly woman answered her door and told the police they were looking for her grandson. She invited them in and gave them access to her grandson's bedroom.

Upon entering the suspect's room, they found the clothing that Danny had identified, a recently fired Ruger on the nightstand and three piles of vomit. Elevated levels of adrenaline in the human body during and after a traumatic event can lead a person to vomit, which is what police surmised is exactly what happened to the suspect.

Although he wouldn't be in custody until the morning after the shooting, police now had a name. A name that was known in the neighborhood to be trouble. The suspect had already served eight months in prison and was now facing charges of, in addition to other accusations, felony possession of a firearm and assault with a deadly weapon.

Danny got to go home that night, but he wasn't allowed to return to work for six weeks. During that time, he received counseling and tried to understand how a jaywalking stop turned into something so traumatic. There were nightmares, flashbacks and the traditional signs of PTSD. For Danny, dealing with the aftermath of the shooting was especially difficult.

The coming weeks were stressful. Danny felt isolated and surrounded by people who didn't understand what he was going through. How was he to talk to his family and friends about such a dangerous situation? How could he convey his feelings to them when he couldn't understand them himself?

Firing his weapon became a mental burden laced with judgment and speculation. There were also supporters who glamorized the situation. In truth, it's neither glamorous nor something that should be judged. It wasn't until Danny was able to return to work that he felt he could talk freely about the incident. He was surrounded by people who understood his choice to shoot instead of walk away. It was then that Danny felt the burden start to lift and normalize.

As a Catholic, he believes "Thou Shalt Not Kill". Seems counter-intuitive for a police officer, doesn't it? It's not. A police officers job is not to kill. It's not in the job description and it never will be. Danny's only thought at the time was "I need to stop this threat." There were innocent people nearby, there was no anger, no hatred, just the sight of a gun barrel pointed at him. The only way Danny could stop the suspect from firing gun was to use his weapon.

It was months before Danny could accept his decision and reconcile it with his Catholic faith. He hadn't been to confession in some time and felt he had more to confess than usual. He also needed to talk to the priest about the shooting, to try to make peace with his decisions and actions. The conversation took so long, his wife, who was waiting for him, became concerned. When Danny finally emerged from the confessional, he looked as though he had been crying.

It's been six years since the shooting and Danny still breaks down when he tells about his meeting with the priest. Danny lived with his guilt, believing he had done something for which he couldn't be forgiven, for 8 months. He had taken an action that seemed to be completely against everything he believed. In that moment, he believed he had wanted to kill someone and that the only way he could survive and prevent harm to the people around him was to stop the attacker with a bullet. Knowing this was something Danny just could not understand or accept.

Fortunately for Danny, the priest was able to help him reconcile his actions with his beliefs. He was doing what was expected in the line of duty, trying to protect himself and others from the threat of death. Danny realized that "sometimes you have to make the decision to take a life. It's not something I want to do." It took more than a confession to move forward. Danny spent a lot of time talking and seeking help. But the confession was what he needed to forgive himself, an important step in healing and moving forward.

When asked if he was ready to make the same decision, Danny said he is. He knows what his responsibilities are as a law enforcement officer; he knows he will stop someone from killing others if he must. As for his feelings around being shot at, being the victim, he was angry and scared. But he said, "I signed up for it." Danny knows that death is one of the risks of his job, but he also didn't sign up to die. He signed up to protect. That's what he was doing that day. He was protecting the people in the truck, his cadet and the people in the surrounding apartments.

Sometimes protecting means making a decision you'd rather not make.

Ken Jefferson
Married
5 Children, 1 Dog
Sworn In 1986
Retired Florida Police Officer
Favorite Ice Cream – Vanilla

CHAPTER SEVENTEEN

KEN

At 6" tall, Ken has a formidable appearance. Put on a badge and a uniform, he appears more authoritative. But once you look into his face and hear him speak, you know that Ken's height isn't the only thing that sets him above others. He is kind, compassionate, soft-spoken and, when telling a story, he states the first and last names of every person he discusses. He doesn't just re-member their names; he remembers them, his encounter with them, what they were experiencing and how he interpreted the situation so he could facilitate the best possible outcome. Whether you are heading to jail, or being pulled over for speeding, Ken's long arm is the law that you want to see.

Growing up in a family with seven kids, Ken saw that stable supervision and understanding was key to keeping order. Anything less, would result in chaos and someone getting into trouble. Even during the difficult times, losing their home, eating baloney sandwiches and doing his homework in the back of a station wagon, Ken knew that his circumstances shouldn't dictate his behav-ior. No matter how hard things were, it was important to maintain his dignity and help those around him do the same.

Ken's childhood had many defining moments, not all of which came at home. Though you wouldn't know it by looking at him, Ken was bullied as a child. He didn't have much, but what he had – his milk money – was taken from him by a group of kids who would beat him up and throw his school books in the woods. Back then bullying wasn't something that garnered the attention it does today. Ken felt helpless and unsure of what to do. He just wanted to prevent other kids from getting picked on in the future. This was one of the two defining moments that launched his law enforcement career.

The other would be an interaction with a man called "Officer Friendly." Although Ken remembers his real name, the Jacksonville Sheriff's Office called him Officer Friendly. The sheriff's office had established a program that would send officers to local elementary schools to connect with the children in the community.

Growing up in Jacksonville, Ken saw plenty of crime and he had seen many interactions where the police intervention led to arrests. That's not what Officer Friendly wanted the kids to hear about. He wanted them to know that the main role of a police officer is to restore neighborhoods and keep peace. The best part of their job is not arresting people; it's creating a safe environment in which people don't want to commit crimes.

It was at that moment an impressionable fifth grader knew that becoming a public servant, defending those who couldn't defend themselves, was his calling. Ken's eager hand shot up and he asked how he could become a police officer. He became a member of the school safety patrol that week.

Armed with his father's words, "Whatever you do, you be the best. If you're picking up garbage, make people stop and watch you while you dump that can in the truck. Don't let anyone do it better," Ken set out to be the best law enforcement officer he could be.

The road wasn't easy; his car broke down while driving to his first day of the academy. As luck would have it, an officer pulled up behind him, helped him get his car to the side of the road and drove Ken, and his wife, to their destinations. There was no money to fix the car. Ken persevered, getting back and forth without one. He graduated and joined the Jacksonville Sheriff's Office in 1986. His career is riddled with accolades, praise for his leadership, commitment to the community and his work with at-risk youth. His wall is lined with awards. Ken is the only person to be named Florida's Public Information Officer of the Year two years in a row. He's also received the FBI Director's Community Leadership Award, a lifesaving award, and a Community Crisis Award. He's lived up to his father's words.

Throughout his twenty-four year career, Ken has worked in many departments and experienced a lot of emotion. Like many officers, there are a few events that have impacted him more than others.

While working off-duty at the 2002 Jacksonville Fair, Ken was preparing to go home when he heard a loud crash. Two cars had collided and one of them landed in a retention pond. Ken immediately ran to the shoreline. On a cold November night, as the car began to sink, a teenaged girl freed herself from the car and began swimming to shore. Initial relief turned to dread as Ken saw three heads pop up and begin crying for help. Trapped in the car, unable to swim, were three girls, two age fourteen and one age eight. Ken immediately threw off his gear and shoes and swam to the vehicle. After bringing one girl to shore, he went back into the dark frigid water for the others.

Consumed by fear, the girls jumped onto Ken hoping he would hold them up, but they pushed him under. When he re-surfaced, they grabbed hold of him again and again he found himself beneath the dark cold water. By now, he feared for his own life and began thinking about his wife and child, how they would manage without him. In a world of split-second decisions, Ken decided it would be best if he swam away from the girls and then tried to get them to shore. He resurfaced away from their reach, and instructed one of them to hold onto the car while he dragged the other one to safety.

By the time he reached the shore, about to collapse from hypothermia and exhaustion, Ken was happy to see that another officer was on his way to the third girl. Ken didn't have to go back in, but he would have. The sheer terror in the girls' voices was enough for Ken to know he couldn't leave them. He would give it his all to save them. There was no time to think or rationalize; there was only time to prevent those cries from haunting his dreams at night. The only way to do that was to save them.

Later that night, while standing by his bedside in the hospital, his wife was grateful he had survived. He had taken in a lot of water and needed a tetanus shot. If she was thinking, "you could have drowned", she didn't say it aloud. She told him how proud she was and that she was thankful that he is alive and was able to save the girls' lives.

The other incident that stuck with Ken involved the 1990 shooting death of Officer Warren Corway Sanders. Officer Sanders was what Ken called a "policeman's policeman." He was a military vet, a tough but fair cop, and treated everyone with respect, even the people he arrested. While heading in for his shift, Ken heard the radio come alive with chatter from the brass, men who wouldn't normally be on the radio at eleven at night. Although he thought it was odd, he didn't know what was going on and no details were discussed.

In those days, 100 officers would fill a room for roll call. Each night this group of men and women would come together to share greetings and stories before heading out on their routes. This night would hold no laughter or tall tales.

"We regret to inform you that Officer Warren Sanders was shot and killed earlier this evening."

An undercover assignment had gone bad costing Officer Sanders his life and putting his partner in the hospital with multiple gunshot wounds. Although the partner would survive, Ken's sense of normalcy was shattered. Anger, hurt and frustration took hold immediately. Their friend, comrade and brother had just been senselessly gunned down. Ken suddenly realized how lucky they were to safely make it home from their shift each night. He also realized just how lucky he was; the brotherhood of support reached out to the Jacksonville Sheriff's Office and offered the comfort they needed. It also reminded Ken that he will never be alone.

Ken also wanted to be sure his family was never alone. He became more thankful and more vigilant. When his children asked why their Dad couldn't get a job that would allow him to be home on nights and weekends, Ken made sure he spent as much time as he could with them. If the job was ever going to take him from them, he wanted to make sure they never forgot him.

After 24 years, his retirement was bittersweet. He would miss the camaraderie more than the hustle and bustle. The children he had watched grow up were now men and women in the community that he loved. Jacksonville was seeing a new generation of lives that were hoping for a stable police force to keep the peace and restore their neighborhoods. For Ken, this meant his career wasn't over. His wife and five children are his biggest supporters in his race for Sheriff. He can't seem to give up the calling he has felt since the age of ten.

Ken has a unique qualification in his race for sheriff, and something that we can all benefit from. His wisdom. When Ken asked me what an officer's most powerful weapon is, I had no idea. His words are something I will not forget.

"Discretion is the most power that an officer has. They can give you a ticket, or give you a warning. They've got discretion with regard to minor offenses, but there's not a lot of latitude when it comes to blatant crimes. Not everyone has to go to jail. If discretion is used properly, an officer will be respected and successful. When they build relationships, discretion comes easily."

Cheryl Finnegan
Widow
2 Dogs
Favorite Ice Cream – Chocolate

CHAPTER EIGHTEEN

CHERYL

David and Cheryl's relationship began the same way it ended, by accident. While he was a grad student, David shared a house with an old friend of Cheryl's; they met when she was picking up her friend for a bridal shower. When the wedding date approached, Cheryl's date backed out and she was set up with David. The wedding date turned into another wedding date – theirs.

David was an intelligent, caring man. He received his undergraduate degree from The Citadel while on a naval ROTC scholarship, then a graduate degree from Worcester Polytechnic Institute. He was a naval officer during the first Gulf War, and had a career as a fire protection engineer at the Idaho National Laboratory. None of that would matter to Gem Lake, Mother Nature, or the police force that set out to find him. To the lake and Mother Nature, he was another being caught in its wintery grasp. To the police force, he was a man who needed to be rescued, at all costs.

David and Cheryl moved to Idaho as a fresh start. Having lived in the same place where they grew up, they both thought it was time for a change. David needed to find a place he could enjoy the outdoors and be the person he wanted to be, not who he was expected to be. He found that in Idaho Falls and spent eighteen months doing just that. The couple enjoyed day trips to historic places and national parks. They even adopted two Labrador Retrievers to make their small family complete.

David loved their dogs, Murray and Jazz. He especially loved taking them for long walks along Gem Lake. It was a beautiful walk and the dogs enjoyed it. Friday, December 9, 2011, the couple planned to eat dinner at their favorite Thai restaurant before addressing Christmas cards. 2011 was the first year David and Cheryl had created photo Christmas cards. Those cards were the only pictures of Cheryl, David and the dogs. It would be a bittersweet memento. While Cheryl was getting ready, David, Murray, and Jazz headed out for their walk.

After an hour had passed, Cheryl became a little concerned but thought perhaps David had stopped to pick something up on the way home. After two hours, panic set in. It was a cold winter night and David should have been back. After trying his phone twice – one call going to voicemail, the other not going through at all – Cheryl got into her car and headed to Gem Lake. Her initial fear was that she wouldn't find the lake. By now it was dark and she had only been there once. The lake was David's spot with the dogs.

On her way there, her heart pounded and her body began to react to the stress. Being stuck behind a train didn't help; it only delayed her time in reaching the lake. As she approached, she saw Murray and Jazz walking down the road with no leashes. They were wet, cold and dejected. She loaded them into the car, they crawled up together in the back seat and looked forlorn. Cheryl knew from the dogs' behavior something was terribly wrong. Three feet later, she found their frozen harness.

It was then she knew the dogs had been in the lake. She called 911.

After the 911 dispatcher took her information, Cheryl was told a unit was on the way and it would be best if she got in touch with a friend so she would have some support. The first officer arrived while her friend was leaving his house.

When an officer arrives on scene, his first responsibility is to find out the facts and gather as much information as possible so he can offer the appropriate response quickly. Cheryl explained what had happened. The officer called for backup and began to look for David. Cheryl was instructed to sit in her friend's car, away from the lake so that she would not be a witness if they found anything that would be upsetting to her. It was now seven o'clock at night.

For the next six hours, crews arrived, a helicopter summoned, spotlights set up and a ground search conducted. Although the officers believed it would be a recovery operation, they treated is as though it was a rescue so they had every resource available to save David, if that was an option. In the meantime, Cheryl felt in her heart that David was gone. The condition of the dogs told her something terrible had happened.

By two o'clock, the officer assigned to support Cheryl told her she should go home and get some sleep. It was cold and there was nothing she could do, she would need her strength over the coming days. Cheryl was on emotional overload. The love of her life was somewhere in the cold and she could not help him. Her mind was also working overtime. When she looks back now, she is able to laugh at what happened next. At the time it seemed perfectly appropriate. She asked the officer if she needed to go to the station first. "I know from watching TV that the spouse is always a suspect. Are you going to need to question me?" The gentleness and under-standing in the officer's voice, assuring her they knew it was an accident, struck Cheryl on a profound level. Having never dealt with law enforcement in this capacity, she had no idea what to expect. All she knew is that she was overcome with grief and the officers on the scene offered her a lifeline.

Cheryl arrived the next morning at eight and she was amazed at what she found. "The night of the accident they enlisted all of their available resources, volunteers, spotlights, and two helicopters in hopes of finding him alive. The following morning sixty-plus people combed the area on foot and quad-pods. They found a plane-spotter to fly over in case they could see something in the ice, along with a remote sub to search below the surface. The river feeds a reservoir downstream, which would have meant having to open a bypass at the falls bringing the possibility of his body being swept away, and they lobbied to delay that as long as possible."

There were over sixty volunteers searching on foot and ATVs. It was then Cheryl learned that many of them had lost loved ones to the lake. Some of the officers had not only lost someone they loved, but they had fallen in during previous rescue attempts. The fact that these people put their personal fears and feelings aside to find her husband touched her deeply.

While rescuers were hoping for a miracle, family had arrived from Massachusetts and were standing with Cheryl. At noon, she was again sent home to have lunch and warm up. While there, her assigned Deputy arrived with ominous news. They had found David's hat and earmuffs and the dogs' leashes in the water. They were able to piece together what they believed had happened.

It appeared that the dogs somehow got loose and onto the ice. David performed search and rescue in the

Navy and had crawled across the ice on his stomach to rescue the dogs. Because he knew not to walk on the ice, there were no footprints so they could not track where he had gone in. This was not a surprise to Cheryl. She knew that the dogs never would have left David if they had a choice. She also knew how strong David's love was for the Murray and Jazz and that he would do anything to save them.

Over the next few weeks, daily searches were conducted on different parts of the river. Although the officers dressed appropriately, the situation was extremely dangerous. When two of them fell through the ice, Cheryl and the Lieutenant agreed that it was best to call off the search. The risk of injury to the officers searching was too high. They all knew that David was gone. Despite this, the officers had a job to do. David needed to be brought home. During breaks in the frigid weather, teams would go out and continue the search. They had a responsibility to Cheryl, to anyone that needed them, and they were going to fulfill it.

What resonated with Cheryl was the response she received and the sacrifice people were willing to make for a regular guy in Idaho Falls. She never expected that. "They really pulled out all the stops," she said. "I was amazed at all of the volunteers and work that the officers did. Not a week went by without someone coming by to tell me they were still doing everything they could."

A pilot was enlisted to fly up and down the river to try and spot anything abnormal on the ice. After a young boy lost his life on the river, a remote control submarine was donated in his memory to help with future rescue efforts. The sub spent hours in the water trying to find David. So many little gestures added up to one large feeling of comfort for Cheryl.

She was also grateful for the compassion the searchers showed. The first morning, Cheryl was sitting in the car when a reporter came over and knocked on the window. The reporters would not take no for an answer, and Cheryl didn't want to talk to them. It took much too long for them to go away. The moment the officers found out what had happened, they contacted the local station and told them to leave her in peace. The next day, when the media van showed up, the police made it clear that the reporters had to deal with the people at the sheriffs' office, not the victim's family. The officers' understanding of her need for privacy and respect for her grief was another act Cheryl felt she could never repay.

"In addition to pulling out all the stops, and then some, they worked very hard to keep the press at bay," she said. "It is unimaginable that they (the media) would try to ambush a family in their worst possible moment, and the officers went out of their way to prevent that. There were no personal details leaked, and my husband's privacy was completely respected."

For three months, officers searched for David, kept Cheryl updated, and offered her what little comfort they could. On March 10, 2012, David was found. Cheryl was standing in the middle of Chicago's O'Hare airport when she received the call. In a split second, she was transported back to the beginning of the grief cycle and she began to sob. Travelers passed by going about their business, not knowing that she had lost her husband for a second time.

When Cheryl arrived home, the Lieutenant brought her David's belongings and he thanked her for making things easy for them. Cheryl was a realist; she knew long ago that David was gone and that he would be found when the time was right. She had no expectation and she knew that people were making sacrifices to find him.

The Lieutenant was grateful that Cheryl had treated them with the same respect they had given her. They appreciated her attitude and support.

Once David was found, a memorial service was held. In lieu of flowers, Cheryl asked that donations be made to the local search and rescue for more equipment so that next time those responsible for the search would be able to do just a little more.

As part of her mourning process, Cheryl wrote *Left Behind: A Guide for Survivors and Their Loved Ones*. It was published in 2014. Many people asked Cheryl questions after David's death. Others wanted to but didn't know how. While people were searching for David, Cheryl had a set of issues to deal with that she never knew about. Amongst other legal problems, she lost her health insurance because David was missing not dead. The book became a journal and a resource for her, and a guide to prevent others from suffering through the things one never thinks about.

When asked why she contacted me about this book she said, "I think what you're doing is admirable and important given how difficult their (the police's) job is. A few bad apples harped on in the press really makes it tough for them. They risked their lives despite the fact that David could no longer be helped. On a more personal level, they were very sympathetic as many had also lost relatives in that river over the years. They offered not only professional, but personal support if I needed anything at all. I have nothing but praise for their efforts to bring me closure."

Cheryl wanted to share her story in the hope that someone reads it and realizes that law enforcement is a deeply personal profession and the lives and emotions of the officers are on the line every day. In their effort to serve the public, they put their own physical and emotional safety at risk time and again.

Brian E.
Married
2 Children, 2 Dogs
Active Since 2012
Pennsylvania Police Officer
Favorite Ice Cream – Orange Sherbet

CHAPTER NINETEEN

BRIAN E

Sometimes it's the people we don't meet that make the greatest impressions on us, and that was the case for Brian. Brian's 'Grandpap' was the most popular guy in prison. He wasn't an inmate giving out free cigarettes; he was a law enforcement officer who spent 20 years working at a state prison in Pennsylvania, loving every moment of it. He was a good-natured man who treated the prisoners with respect and kindness. When Grandpap was 45-years-old, his dream of becoming a New Mexico State Trooper was about to come true. Unfortunately, he died from a sudden brain aneurysm. Not many prisoners set aside a day to mourn the death of a guard, but this group did. Grandpap was respected and this was shown through a day of mourning throughout the prison.

This was the reason Brian became a police officer. He never met Grandpap but, as a child, Brian heard stories of him, and his love and respect for the law. Lacking a solid father figure, Grandpap became the person Brian wanted to emulate. He wanted to help people and enter a profession that he believed was an anchor in society, one that provided role models and protected the public.

Sometimes the path to our dreams is not easy, and being a law enforcement officer is no different. You don't just wake up one day and put on the uniform. You need training, equipment and a job. It's expensive and time-consuming. It's much like college, and you often have to pay for it yourself. Not having the money to put himself through the academy early in life, Brian waited.

Eventually, he married and his wife saw his deep desire to fulfill his dream. They worked together on a budget and were able to put him through the academy with a little bit of personal sacrifice. Brian is now an officer and they still make sacrifices. Many police departments in his area pay $9-12 per hour, offer no benefits, and officers have to provide all of their own gear. This is not uncommon in law enforcement. But for many, the love of the job is such they make the sacrifices and hard choices.

In addition to his love of law, Brian is also a dog lover and a sympathetic guy. While responding to a call of a stray dog "menacing" the streets of Pennsylvania, he found an eight-pound Shih Tzu. He was no stranger to this vicious beast. The dog belonged to a home Brian had frequented for domestic violence calls. Finding no one at home, Brian needed to make a decision. Choices are made daily as a police officer, and some are more difficult than others. Some are made in a split second and some occasions offer more time to think.

Brian didn't need a lot of time to think about what to do. This was a home where domestic violence had occurred; who knew what would happen if the family had to go to the pound and pay a fee? Did Brian really need to turn the dog in? No, he didn't. He knew that the evening of the woman and child living in the home would go a lot smoother if he let the dog hang around with him until they got home. It was one time he knew they would be happy to come to the police station.

With his imposing new partner in the car, Brian made a traffic stop. While speaking to the woman, his "partner" began barking, apparently feeling larger than his size surrounded by the authority of a police vehicle. Surprised to see such a small dog in a police car, the woman asked if there was really a Shih Tzu in his cruiser. Not missing a beat, Brian replied that the borough had a vicious new K-9. They both had a good laugh and she was free to go with a warning. Two good deeds in one day. As simple as they seem, they make the day a lot easier when an officer can help people rather than arrest them. These are events officers look forward to.

Later in the day, after receiving the message that the Shih Tzu was safely in Brian's care, the relieved mother and daughter arrived at the station to pick him up - the dog, not Brian. The mother was extremely grateful and her five-year-old daughter hugged Brian tightly and thanked him for "saving" her dog. Brian did have to write up the incident and some things just can't be kept quiet in rural Pennsylvania. He became known for miles around as the first and only officer with a K-9 Shih Tzu. It's safe to say Grandpap would be proud.

Pamela Barnum
Married
1 Child
Sworn In 1994
Retired Detective Ontario Provincial Police
Favorite Ice Cream – Caramel Fudge

CHAPTER TWENTY

PAM

Police work in Canada is much the same as in the United States, and people join the police force for many of the same reasons. As a child, Pam listened to her uncle, a staff sergeant with the Ontario Provincial Police, tell his stories. It didn't take long before she knew what she wanted to do. Following his advice, she went to university before pursuing her career in police work.

Pam joined the Ontario Provincial Police, Canada's second largest police service, in 1994 as a constable. After three years, she transferred to the drug enforcement section as a detective. She became only the second woman in a unit of 89 officers. As daunting as that sounds, Pam took it in stride. She knew it would be challenging, and, at times, it was. She would never be "one of the boys," but she proved herself capable early on through professionalism and hard work, and was able to earn the respect of everyone she worked with.

Pam spent nine years in the drug unit as an undercover officer, and adjustments to the lifestyle and way of thinking were difficult at first. One cannot just assume a new name and walk into a new life on the street. The prep work is tedious. There can be no slip-ups and the fear of being discovered must be overcome. Imagine leaving your house knowing it will be months before you return. During those months, you will have to pretend you are someone else, and if you make a mistake there is a chance you will die. You initially live in fear, but, over time, you stop looking over your shoulder and adapt to your new role. If you don't adjust, the paranoia will consume you and you will get caught. Police work is a constantly changing environment. New skills are learned daily, and undercover work was no different. You just have to learn things more quickly.

On one particular project that lasted ten months, Pam was able to earn the trust of the people she was investigating so quickly that one subject asked her to stand up with her in her wedding. "There is always something in the back of your mind that one day you are going to reveal who you truly are. For some (like the woman with the wedding) I felt bad about destroying her sense of trust in people. She had a difficult life, and although she made really poor choices (selling cocaine), she was not a bad person at her core."

Another woman fell into dealing cocaine by circumstance. Living around drugs and trusting the wrong people can turn your life into something you may not have expected. Sue was an example of this. She was lonely, vulnerable, and accepted the first hand that reached out to her. Before she could realize her mistake, she was in too deep. While recovering from leukemia, Sue needed help paying her rent and had no family. She allowed one of her "friends" to help financially and drive her to the hospital for treatment. When she recovered, Sue found out what all of that "help" would really cost: the friend expected payback in the form of help with his drug business.

Sue started transporting drugs as a mule and eventually moved on to become a dealer. Before she knew it, she was dealing multiple ounces of cocaine every day. Pam spent a lot of time with Sue, becoming her friend and confidant. That's part of the job: getting people to trust you regardless of what you feel for the people or the circumstances. As Sue and Pam became friends, Pam met Sue's cat, a pet that meant everything to Sue. The cat was the only being that loved her unconditionally and expected nothing in return.

A few months later, Sue was evicted from her apartment and couldn't take her cat to her new apartment. Because Pam had developed a meaningful relationship with Sue, she asked Pam to look after her cat. With only one week until takedown and a soft spot for animals, Pam took the cat to her undercover apartment. Eventually, the cat went to live with one of Sue's friends, but not until the night before Pam revealed her true identity.

Although Pam knew that her job was to bring down Sue and everything she represented, Sue and the cat were still living beings. Times like these are difficult for officers. They know they have to accept their roles and they aren't there to make friends; they are working to get drug dealers off the street. But once in a while, someone comes along and the officer can't help but feel bad for them. Sue was one of those people. Deep down she was a decent person who happened to be doing really stupid things. These were the people that Pam hoped eventually got the help they needed to free themselves from their addictions and their illegal activities. In getting drug dealers off the street, these are the people Pam saves from becoming just another statistic.

Takedown day is the day the undercover officers arrest all of the people who sold them drugs, and the protocol is to introduce themselves as undercover police officers while wearing a suit and a badge. It's not a fun day. Many of the subjects become angry and threatening while others hold a silent respect for the officer's ability to fool them. Very few thank the officers. Sue was one of those people. She told Pam, "Thank you for being kind and helping me. I am going to change."

It was an especially poignant moment for Pam, and she had mixed emotions. Sue had grown to trust Pam. In return, Pam misled her, she had no choice. It's tough realizing that not everyone an officer encounters is a hardcore criminal who deserves no mercy. At the same time, Pam was proud of the job she had done. Their project resulted in the arrests of over sixty drug dealers.

Pam later heard that Sue had, in fact, turned her life around. She had gotten a full-time job, was no longer selling cocaine, and completed rehab. Pam still thinks about Sue and people like her, the people who are able to turn things around as a result of Pam's work. "That's why we do the job we do," she said. "It's not about right and wrong - it's about community; working together to have safe and healthy communities."

For the majority of subjects she has taken down, Pam didn't have a lot of empathy to spare. Takedown day was something she looked forward to. By and large, drug dealers are not good people and many made it their daily mission to destroy lives. Those were the ones Pam loved to look in the face while she revealed her true identity. Those were the days that Pam knew what she was doing was worth it; the fear for her own safety was worth the outcome.

Though she enjoyed notifying drug dealers that she was a police officer, there were people she never wanted to give bad news to, like the couple whose child, spouse, and two grandchildren were all killed in a traffic accident. In mere moments, a family is wiped out – a mother, a father, and their two children. In what seemed to take hours longer than it actually did, Pam had to notify the grandparents of the accident and escort them to the hospital to identify their only child with the spouse and the only grandchildren they had.

Pam wasn't prepared for that; there is no training for those moments. Your heart breaks along with those of the victims and the families. You are a prop in the worst moment of their lives. They will try to forget you, but they never will. You hope that you can erase their pain-filled wails from your mind, but you never will. You are now bound together by tragedy, but you cannot express your emotion in front of them.

Pam remained compassionate and professional. She didn't want the elderly couple see her cry. She didn't want them to bear her grief as well as theirs. Instead, she spent part of her shift in the women's washroom crying. As a young, female police officer, she didn't want anyone to see her cry. She didn't want anyone to know that the pain of her task was great enough to break her game face. She didn't want anyone to think she was too feminine for the job. As years passed, Pam learned it is okay to cry, your game face will sometimes shatter, and the only thing you have to overcome is your own ego. Police work will wreak havoc on your emotions and you have to let it out. Everyone at the station understands because they've all been there.

Because they've all had the same experiences, there is a camaraderie associated with policing that Pam loved and now misses. When she became pregnant with her son, she decided that it was best if she found a safer job. As a police officer, you are often expected to put your job first. You have to give 100% when you are working because you must keep yourself and those around you safe.

Pam was honest with herself; she knew that she wanted to be a mother before she was a police officer. It was a difficult choice that was made easier by the fact that she had already made a difference in more than one life.

Ray Leeth
Single
3 Horses
Active Since 2013
Virginia Police Officer
Favorite Ice Cream – Cookies and Cream

CHAPTER TWENTY-ONE

RAY

Compassion, and physical and emotional toughness, are required when working as an Emergency Room Technician. Those qualifications are also needed in law enforcement. Ray is able to transition between both. When he isn't working in an ER, he is volunteering as an officer with his local police department.

At the age of 25, despite his degree in Criminal Justice and his graduation from the police academy, Ray still has a lot to learn. One hot summer night, a man in a wheelchair reminded him just how much.

Responding to a call for a man who seemed out of place, Ray and his partner met a remarkable man named Jim. Jim was from Oregon. After his house had burned down, he decided to pack up what little he had left and travel to meet family in Florida. As they talked, Ray found out that Jim was traveling with a few dollars in his pocket and a bag of tools to repair his vehicle as needed. When he ran short on cash, Jim would find work along the way and fill his pockets until he needed more. At the age of 61, this hardly seems remarkable or out of place. Lots of people head south in their twilight years.

What made Jim stand out from the crowd was the fact that he was traveling in a wheelchair and passersby were concerned for his safety being so close to the road. When Jim left Oregon, he had both legs. Somewhere in his journey he was hit by a car and lost one of them. What's even more remarkable is that Jim had been on the road for three years, three months and three weeks. He was literally taking the long way home. Not many people think that Virginia is a direct route from Oregon to Florida.

What struck Ray was the incredible sense of humor and positive attitude that Jim possessed. At 61, Jim decided to see the country, in his own time and his own way before settling back down. Jim had had a difficult life; he won his battle against alcoholism, had seen a lot of death in his family and decided that he was going to enjoy the rest of his years. For him, that meant enjoying his trip. He had a goal and he planned to complete it.

Ray and his partner were happy to offer Jim a ride that night. They drove him about 40 miles to the next county, filled his backpack with supplies, added lights to the back of his wheelchair and wished him well. Jim was so appreciative of their kindness, his eyes welled with tears.

That night, Ray learned that no matter what condition a person is in, no matter what has happened to them along the way, what matters most is keeping your sense of humor and a positive attitude. During the car ride, Jim regaled them with stories of his travels and lessons in life. Ray took a lot of it to heart. He couldn't imagine losing his leg and continuing his journey, fulfilling his dream of backpacking cross-country. Ray always tries to be as honest and helpful as possible. Because of Jim, he realizes that no matter how small his gesture, it is deeply appreciated.

As for becoming an officer, it was something he knew he wanted to do as a child, with an uncle in the FBI and friends and family in law enforcement, his favorite Halloween costume was a police officer. As soon as he could afford to put himself through the academy, he did. What he doesn't realize is that he is a lot like Jim. He had a dream; he waited, made a plan and is now working toward his own goal.

Walter
Married
1 Child, 2 Cats
Sworn In 1968
Retired Connecticut Police Officer
Favorite Ice Cream – Cherry Garcia

CHAPTER TWENTY-TWO

WALTER

Walter means "powerful warrior." People with this name desire a stable, loving family or community, and have a need to work with others. Walter is a powerful warrior – not with a weapon, but with his mind and his heart. His parents unknowingly gave him a name with a meaning he would uphold each day of his career. The stability he offered his family and community is something from a storybook. When searching for subjects for this book I knew I would find men and women with a life so well led, people we can all respect. Walt is one of them.

When Walt was a kid, his father installed radios in cars at the local police departments and performed other communications work. This enabled him to establish lasting, valuable relationships with law enforcement. Back in those days, the cop on the corner had no trouble tapping Walt's behind with his nightstick as Walt skittered past when he had gotten in trouble at school.

It was a simpler time and the police wore many hats. They carried ropes in their cars to recover loose horses, checked the homes of vacationing residents, delivered news of deceased loved ones to family members, acted as school crossing guards when necessary, and directed commuter traffic every evening from the train station. Although the world has gotten too big for the police to continue all of these practices, there are some things that never change.

His childhood experiences made a lasting impression, and Walt knew that he wanted to serve his country and his community in some way. Initially, he joined the Navy. He received his basic training at Great Lakes Naval Training Center near Chicago and later transported Marines to Panama where they were all trained in jungle survival. The structure, the discipline and the service were something he felt he was meant for. Unfortunately, married life disagreed.

Walt was often away and it was taking a toll on his young bride. Because his marriage was more important he left the Navy after four years. Afterward, he got a job in a large manufacturing company, but discovered that was not something he wanted to do for the rest of his life. He had a friend who had joined the police force, and, having always respected the law, it wasn't hard to convince Walt to join their ranks. Convincing his wife was difficult. It meant taking a pay cut and entering a dangerous, unpopular profession, something for which she was not ready. Luckily, she was supportive. She understood and knew his sacrifice would be greater than hers if he could not do what he believed he was called to do.

His daughter, Sandy, was a year old when he became a police officer. As she grew to understand his chosen career, she couldn't have been prouder. She was so proud that she offered to help in any way she could. It wasn't enough that she went to the station once a week holding Daddy's hand, or that she knew every officer's name and they knew hers. She wanted to do more. When Walt eventually took over the Marine Division, Sandy, age 12, was at the ready. She would pretend to drown while the officers 'saved' her, put her on a backboard and brought her in. In exchange, she learned CPR and continued the tradition her Dad had started when he was a child; the tradition that involves love and respect for the men and women who patrol our streets.

Ironically, the incident that struck Walt the hardest was his first drowning, and Amy Brown's name is forever carved into his heart. In March 1969, four short months after being sworn in as a police officer in Connecticut, Walt responded to a call for a missing four-year-old girl. Other than cute kittens, nothing touches more hearts than the innocence and purity of children. Each time an officer is called out for a missing child, he might as well be on a roller coaster. His heart falls into his stomach, and a range of emotions plays through him as he wonders what he will find.

Because of a fresh snowfall, Walt could easily follow the girl's tracks down to the pond where he could see her floating face down in a hole in the ice. He doesn't remember thinking about what to do. He threw down his gear, removed his shoes and made his way onto the ice. It broke under his weight and he swam to Amy, knowing in his heart she was already gone. Despite his attempts at CPR, she vomited her lunch but no breath would ever make its way through her body again.

Nothing anyone will ever tell you can prepare you for that kind of call. There is no course at the police academy that tells you how you will feel when you hold a dead child in your arms. Nothing that will convince you that 35 years later you can close your eyes, relive the entire incident and vividly remember the contents of her stomach, always knowing her last meal. Nothing that can prepare you for that fear, the fear of hearing her mother wailing behind you. The fear of having to tell her mother that she is gone once you stop CPR.

While Walt was wet and shivering in 30-degree weather, trying desperately to bring Amy back, the ambulance and his supervisors had arrived. They took over life-saving attempts and brought the mother to the hospital where they could break the news to her in a more controlled environment. Walt was left to drive 24 miles in a freezing uniform, to walk up his front steps and tell his wife why he was home, to hug his then two-year-old daughter and go back out on patrol once he was clean and dry.

What he wanted more than anything was to cry: for the child, for the mother, for every man or woman who tries to breathe a false life into a lifeless body. To cry because it's so hard to face the reality. Because they are the first responders, they are supposed to save lives. Sometimes they can't.

But sometimes they can. One evening, Walt was working at a local tavern and witnessed a terrible accident. A 28-year-old woman was walking between parked cars to enter the tavern when another car, traveling at a high rate of speed, hit the line of cars, pinning the woman between them. Both her legs were severed just above the knee. She was conscious the entire time.

Walt was the first one on the scene while the blood literally drained from the gaping wounds. Thinking quickly, Walt fashioned tourniquets with by-standers' belts in an effort to prevent the woman from bleeding out on the street. He held her hand, trying to make her believe that she would be fine, hoping that she could stay alert long enough to be saved. By the time the paramedics arrived, the woman had formed a bond with Walt and was terrified of him leaving her side. Walt rode with her to the hospital and stayed until she was brought into surgery. Knowing that it would be hours before she was conscious, Walt washed up and returned to his post. Because that is what cops do.

Compelled by a concern for her well-being, Walt and his wife, Jan, visited the young lady in the hospital the next day. She was pleased to see him and grateful for what he had done. Most people don't understand, but when you go through something that traumatic and personal, it creates a bond. The visit gave them both the closure they needed. Police go through these types of experiences on a regular basis; they create many bonds. Like it or not, they represent a lifeline for so many people.

Not a lot of people like working for a living, but we choose a career path, with its ups and downs, and we can usually leave it behind. It doesn't seep into the crevices of our minds and home life. Police work can do that. Walt, and many like him, learn ways to cope. They are not cold, heartless and emotionless; they learn when they can and can't display their emotions. They have to be able to get up the next day knowing that they may witness a death, abuse, or cruelty. The only way to do that is by shielding themselves from the pain and horror. They go to the next call, and the next, and the next. There is no break. There is no warm welcome when they arrive on the scene.

More often than not, they are alone; there isn't enough money to staff a police force where everyone can have a partner. Shifts can get long and lonely when you are driving around thinking about the last call, the next call, or whether or not you should call for back up when pulling over a car. There is no water cooler to gather around and no chatter from the people at the desks around you only the sound of your radio.

There were no radios or cell phones when Walt began his law enforcement career by walking a beat in the center of the town; talk about lonely! Officers had to run down the street to the call box to request backup. They could then wait or go back to the scene of the crime. Once he was assigned to a patrol car, there was one time he wished he had waited for a backup, as he should have. As he was chasing an intruder on the second floor of a vacant building, Walt was pushed out a second floor window. The building had once been a sanatorium. The perpetrator knew he could get away quicker if Walt was incapacitated, so he pushed Walt out of a second-floor window.

Push a guy out a window? Walt wasn't a "guy," he was a "pig"; demonstrations were commonplace, and, more often than not, his small-town force wasn't trained for them. A strike by the 50 employees of the local nursing home seemed like something they could handle, but with only 60 miles between their town and New York City, the strike became something much more. Six buses full of protestors arrived and they had a full-scale demonstration on their hands. Headquarters sent more men to cover the crowd. There was apprehension on both sides, but at the end of the day only law enforcement was negatively portrayed. Holding your head high became more and more difficult. But Walt kept coming back, his head held high.

In Walt's third year of service, a car struck him at an accident scene and both his legs were crushed. Because of the injuries, he was in and out of work several times throughout his career. Despite the pain, Walt did whatever he could to continue on in the department. Walt was made for the job and it was a part of who he was and still is. He wanted to be part of a group that, even in those days, was persecuted and lacked support.

After seven years on road patrol, his past injury brought Walt to the Marine Division. It was the only way he could stay on the job. It was a division no one else wanted, but it was the most stylish. He exchanged his uniform pants for navy blue Bermudas, his gun belt for a smaller weapon, and his police hat for a baseball cap. Since no one else wanted the job, Walt was the man. The only thing he knew about boating was where to get his boat shoes. But he learned, because he loved his work and wanted to remain on the force.

Shortly after the release of the movie *The End*, starring Burt Reynolds, Walt came upon a woman in the middle of Long Island Sound, swimming out further and further from land. Immediately concerned for her safety, he stopped to speak to her. She said that she was going to swim until she exhausted herself and then she would die, just like Burt Reynolds wanted to do in the movie. She struggled when he tried to get her into his boat until he finally grabbed a handful of her hair and pulled her aboard. She was later transported to the state mental hospital where she was legally detained. Much to his surprise, he found her a month later trying to do the same thing. She had just been released and was determined to complete her original plan. After saving her life a second time, Walt never saw her again and often wonders if she succeeded or was able to find enough hope and happiness to withstand the trials of life.

Walt turned a one-man division into one with 17 special service officers and 40 auxiliary officers. But even success couldn't keep him on the job forever. The day came when the surgeon told Walt he couldn't work anymore. He was a man with a mission, a house, a daughter in college, and a wife. He was now moving to Florida with a medical pension and a broken heart. The only thing he could do was cry. Men like Walt are built for service, and with a kind heart, a quick smile and a soft voice, he was the type of officer we all want to see on our street corner. His job did not define him; he defined his job.

Looking back, he can see the pivotal points in his life. Naturally, one of them occurred while he was working. He was called to the scene of a sinking sailboat with a family of four aboard. While rescuing the father, the sailboat went down and pulled Walt into 200 feet of water. He was sinking with the boat and he could not get free. As Walt was certain he was about to die, he heard a voice tell him to remove his gun belt. He did, and he floated to the top. His gun was caught on the mast and would surely have drowned him if he hadn't removed the belt. It was this incident that reminded Walt that he had a calling, that there was more for him than retiring.

Walt still has a mission; service hasn't left him. Years ago, Walt was putting people in prison. Today he is feeding their stomachs and souls. Early in his career, Walt became a Christian; it defined how he treated people and how they treated him. In the mid-80s, on a trip to a prison for a Christian retreat, a Hell's Angels member that Walt had put in jail attended the retreat for the free meal. Instead, he found God and became a church member. This is the calling Walt has now. If he cannot bring peace to society through the prevention of crime, he will do it through the promotion of love and running a food pantry four days a week.

"I am now seventy years old and my family still catches me assessing situations that I think might be dangerous or suspicious," he said. "They say, 'Dad's on duty again!' But a real cop never loses his edge; a real cop always checks his surroundings; a real cop cares about people and tries to help when it's needed. I had another career for twenty years after I left the force, but in my heart of hearts I will always be a cop. When it's really part of who you are, you don't take it off when you give up the uniform. I miss it every day and it will always be the best job I ever had!"

The photo of Walt on his first day in uniform still sits on his wife's bureau, there are 5 full scrap books honoring his 17 years of service, and Walt and his wife, Jan, fill each word with pride when they speak of his career. When I spoke to Walt, he had me on speakerphone and Jan contributed every chance she got. It was easy to visualize him sitting in a chair focusing on the phone and his answers while Jan busied herself in the background, placing her hand on his shoulder as she leaned forward to answer. Their obvious love for each other, after so many years, was heartwarming. In a world where many marriages end in divorce, they were able to keep it together.

Jan didn't want him to join the police force, yet she listened to Walt recount his shift each night. She often couldn't sleep because of what he witnessed, but she polished his badge and sent the love of her life out to protect the love of someone else's. Oftentimes, the person in uniform is not the only one serving the public. It is also the family that waits at home. They serve and sacrifice alongside the person wearing the badge.

The thing about Walt that makes him so memorable? His closing words to me: "I hope that when I get to the gates of Heaven, St. Peter, or whoever is waiting for me, has a badge to give me so I feel at home again."

Stanley Kurtz
Married
2 Children
Active Since 2010
Kansas Deputy
Favorite Ice Cream – Rocky Road

CHAPTER TWENTY-THREE

STANLEY

Good officers know that wearing a badge does not make you any better or worse than the next person. It also does not guarantee respect. The guarantee is that they are in a unique position to help people; they will be on the end of the line when someone calls for help. Stan understands that, he knows that he will set the tone for all of his interactions as soon as he shows up. With a respectful manner, an unassuming charm and a calm, steady voice, Stan wins over almost everyone he comes into contact with.

Because of that, Stan has also earned the respect of his peers. Being chosen as the Deputy of the Year is an honor. Being chosen twice, a greater honor. Having an overwhelming majority of the vote both times, you are doing something spectacular, especially when you have only been on the job five years and the award has only been in existence for two. Stan doesn't see it that way. He is just doing his job, treating people with respect and kindness. He attributes his success to his late start. Although he has always dreamed about going into law enforcement, he waited.

"I do not regret waiting to get into this field. I do think my age has given me a level of maturity, allowing me to care, love, help and reach out to my community in positive ways which I don't think I would have had at a younger age. It has allowed me to look at the bigger picture of circumstances rather than what is happening right at the moment, helping me to realize things aren't always as they seem. It has allowed me to see all people as human beings."

His statistics support his outlook. Stan issued only 185 tickets in a year, while he stopped 1,048 people, it's a testament to his calm demeanor and ability to see beyond the situation. He knows that every infraction is different and should be treated independently. Sometimes it's enough to talk to people to find out what is going on.

In the same year, Stan had 172 cases and 94 arrests. One might wonder how Stan can see every one of those interactions as positive and keep him from being jaded. He says it's as easy as being kind. For instance, Stan once saw a motorist with a flat tire and stopped to change it for him. When the motorist, who happened to be a district manager for an auto parts dealer, found out that the sheriff's office did not supply jacks to each of the road deputies and Stan had purchased the jack he used to change tires with his personal money, he made a phone call. The sheriff's department soon found themselves with enough jacks for all of their vehicles as most other deputies did not have one. Stan was just doing what he does, the motorist saw it as something much more and wanted to repay him.

Then there are the bigger deeds he performs, like driving an eighty-eight year old WWII veteran home.

"Probably one of the most memorable times of helping someone was when I had the privilege of helping a

WWII veteran get back home to Broken Arrow, OK. I was on duty and called to help a disoriented elderly man who was at a gas station just northeast of Newton, KS. When I arrived on scene, I was able to determine the elderly man had gone to York, NE to attend a funeral of an old friend. The man had been trying to get home to Broken Arrow, OK for about five days. I immediately knew he was very lost and having a hard time finding his way home. I was also able to obtain he was a WWII veteran and had very little money to get him the rest of the way home. There was no one available (family or friends) to be able to come get him, and I was not comfortable just giving him directions. My shift was to end at seven that evening. As soon as I was officially off duty, my dad and I took a road trip. I drove with the man as my father followed in his vehicle. I had the privilege of spending about three hours with a remarkable eighty-eight-year-old WWII veteran who shared his life story and the sacrifices he made for our Country. My dad and I returned home that next morning around four."

And it's not just adults he loves to help.

"I currently lead an Explorer Program we have created here in Harvey County in recognition of one of our own, Deputy Kurt Ford, who was killed in the line of duty in 2005. It was Kurt's dream to have an Explorer Program. It was made possible and started by a good friend of his and his sister. The Explorer Program is for young people ages 14-20 who are interested in law enforcement. It teaches law enforcement daily routines and how to handle different situations. My kids are a part of that Program and are also involved and like law enforcement."

"Sheriff T. also had 'Honor' cards made for each deputy on our department. The card has a picture of the deputy, with his/her name, and the Sheriff's Department name and logo on the front. On the back, the card shows the deputy's badge number, year they started with the department, hometown, specialty and hobbies. These cards were printed to give to our community as we see fit. I like to give my cards to kids. This gives me an opportunity to talk to the kids, earn a respect and hope they can learn law enforcement are not all about arresting, handing out tickets, and handling what most think of as the bad part of the job."

Stan has an obvious passion for his job; he's found his niche and loves it.

"Although I do like catching 'the bad guys,' the rewards of the job come from just plain helping the average person; helping the single mom with kids in the car who has a flat tire, helping elderly people who have car problems or are lost, just helping people in need. There have been many of times I have bought someone gas or a meal."

As Stan goes about his route, he knows he can't help everyone. Most people must help themselves. People make mistakes and find themselves labeled as a criminal, but they can also learn from those mistakes and turn their lives around. Those are the people who excite Stan the most; they make his job worthwhile. Watching children learn from their parents' mistake and forge better lives for themselves is the most rewarding of all. Like many officers, Stan finds joy in the little things, the things we forget they are doing.

These are the everyday actions that make the job more bearable, the interactions that offset the images of fatalities and abuse. Those images stick with you. It's hard to move on from the tragedy. When the day comes that Stan can't stomach the images anymore, when he doesn't want to go to work or when he acts disrespectfully or gives people attitude, Stan will resign. He knows he will no longer be doing his job to the best of his ability.

Meanwhile, he is a husband and father who knows there are risks with his profession; that he might not come home from his shift. He always gives his wife of twenty-one years and his seventeen-year-old twins a hug and an "I love you" every time he leaves the house. He has no illusions about what he is doing. No amount of respect will take away the danger inherent with the job.

Jeremy Henwood
Deceased
Sworn In 2007
San Diego Police Department

CHAPTER TWENTY-FOUR

JEREMY

When a couple is married, they leave the altar with a sense of hope and excitement for the future, sometimes a plan to have a family. They never walk away thinking that their lives will be disrupted by sadness and tragedy, Bev and Rob Henwood were no different. Their wedding day was full of joy and anticipation, looking forward to beginning their family and new life together.

Sadly, their family would begin and end with tragedy. Their first child, Jeremy, would ironically, be their easiest birth. He was born two weeks late and doctors needed to use forceps during the delivery, but he was a healthy boy. In 1977, their second child would be born at 26 weeks. The hospital did not have a NICU and the child did not survive.

Their next child, Robbie, was also born prematurely, but since they were now in Vancouver and in a hospital with better resources, he was sent home after ten days. Bev and Rob would experience another childbirth loss before they had Emily, slightly premature after months of bed rest, but she was healthy and that's all that mattered. Their family was complete.

Throughout his life, Jeremy earned the respect and love of many people in large part because of his dedication to his country and to the well-being of others. As a young boy, his reputation was slightly different. Born and raised in Canada, it was a surprise to many when Bev and Rob moved Jeremy and Robbie to Texas in 1978, while Rob pursued his career in drug research with his PhD and Beverley followed her medical career. This is where Emily would eventually be born.

At the age of twelve, Jeremy, with an eight-year-old Robbie in tow, snuck out of the house late at night to meet a group of friends to toilet paper a house. The occupant came to the door, chased the kids off and called the police. Jeremy was a bit of an escape artist. While he was returning home, his brother and his friends were taken in by the local police.

Being a matter-of-fact child, he woke the babysitter and asked her to call his parents who were away on a business trip to let them know Robbie was in jail. Looking back, no one would have believed it was a foreshadowing of the fact that Jeremy would always be on the right side of the law explaining things matter-of-factly.

Jeremy's upbringing was a bit on the strict side and as a result, he tended to be rebellious. His parents enrolled him in the Marine Military Academy in Harlingen, Texas. Little did they know this would change Jeremy's life. The Military Academy instilled Jeremy with a deep respect for authority and family.

After graduation in 1995, he enlisted in the United States Marine Corps Reserve. Jeremy completed basic training at the Marine Corps Recruit Depot San Diego and returned to San Antonio to attend the University of Texas where he received his Bachelor of Science degree, majoring in Criminal Justice. Jeremy became a United

States citizen in order to become an officer in the United States Marine Corps.

Jeremy's 15-year military career took him overseas for three tours, two in Iraq and one in Afghanistan. His first two tours in Iraq were served while he was on active duty. In July 2007, he joined the San Diego Police Department and remained a Marine Corps reservist. In August 2010, Marine duty called again and Jeremy was deployed to Afghanistan with the Combat Logistics Regiment 2 as a Bravo Company Commander for Combat Logistics Battalion 2. He was proud to have never lost a man under his command. Selected for promotion to Major in the Marine Reserves, Jeremy returned to San Diego and his police department career in February 2011.

Jeremy spent time in the most dangerous regions of Afghanistan, fighting the Taliban and earning the respect of his fellow Marines. He was a respected leader and carried himself as such. He enjoyed the role of a protector and believed his role in life was to help save others. It was this feeling, buried deep inside, that kept him on duty, that drove him to remain in the military reserves and to choose a parallel career in law enforcement.

During his four-year career with the San Diego Police Department, Jeremy was known as a community-oriented officer. He was strong, emotionally and physically, and could be counted on if you needed back up, a sounding board, or if you were short on cash for lunch. Jeremy was there to help; it was something that was deeply ingrained in him. He also believed in communicating with the people he served, he felt that becoming part of the community was the best way to protect it. Jeremy had a great attitude and was regularly trying to improve himself and other officers.

On August 6, 2011, just six months after returning from Afghanistan, Jeremy was on patrol and stopped at a local McDonalds for a quick dinner. While there, a nine-year-old boy walked nervously behind him, eventually making his way next to Jeremy at the counter. Appearing shy at first, he got up the courage to ask this 6'3" police officer for a few cents to buy a cookie. Rather than give him the money, Jeremy purchased the cookie for the boy and discussed the boy's dream of becoming a police officer or an NBA player when he grows up.

The surveillance video of the interaction has since gone viral, watching it you can see the boy smiling; sometimes shyly, sometimes with laughter and other times with admiration. While discussing life and the future, the piece of advice that stood out the most with the boy was "Hard work in life will do you well." In those moments, a legend was created.

Jeremy left McDonalds to patrol the area around 45th Street and University Avenue when a car flashing its lights approached him from behind. When Jeremy pulled to the curb to assist, the driver produced a shotgun and shot him without warning. The suspect had been involved in another unprovoked shooting in the neighboring city of El Cajon less than a half an hour earlier. An "all units" broadcast of that shooting was being given to SDPD but the suspect shot Jeremy before he could be made aware of the earlier incident, vehicle or suspect description.

While Jeremy was bleeding and holding on to life in his cruiser, the suspect drove off, as did many other drivers. Whether it was out of fear or ignorance of what had happened, some cars drove around Jeremy's cruiser, back into their lives and didn't look back. For others, driving off wasn't an option. Strangers administered first aid, used Jeremy's radio to call for help and gave comfort to a dying man.

Jeremy was rushed to Scripts Mercy Hospital where he died shortly after one a.m., August 7, 2011.

In the meantime, the suspect was surrounded and refused to put down his rifle or surrender. In what was later deemed a 'suicide by cop,' he was killed by officers in the standoff. The witnesses to his shooting couldn't drive away and leave him. They had to remain on scene despite whatever personal feelings they had. A friend and co-worker was clinging to life, as they were tending to the remains of a killer. Once again, there was no rest for their own mental self-preservation. They could not drive away and return to their lives.

Meanwhile, in Texas, Jeremy's parents were enjoying a quiet evening at home when two officers arrived at their doorstep. While Bev went down the hall to grab a robe, she could hear the officers asking Rob to call the number on the card, it was about Jeremy. Bev returned to the living room to talk to the officers while Rob went into the bedroom to make the call.

Most law enforcement families know that if officers arrive at your door, something is terribly wrong. For some reason, Bev didn't make that connection. She thought it was odd that they were there. As they spoke kindly of Jeremy and even hugged her, she thought perhaps Jeremy had shot someone. Either she truly hadn't made the connection, or her subconscious wouldn't let her. Meanwhile, her husband was being told that Jeremy was being kept alive so that they could fulfill his wishes to be an organ donor and they needed permission to do what was necessary.

Rob listened in disbelief at what the doctors were saying. "Shot and injured...not expected to live" was unacceptable. Rob and Bev called the ER doctor three times that night to ask for more information. Jeremy was invincible, so surely they could save him.

Another hour passed and a representative from LifeShare called. They asked questions for at least an hour and then asked to speak with Jeremy's mother as well. This was not supposed to happen. Jeremy was supposed to make these decisions for them not the other way around. It was clear they would not arrive before he was gone so they were asked to decide that night. Surely the worst night ever.

Next, Jeremy's brother Robbie and sister Emily needed to be told. These were the most painful calls the Henwoods have ever had to make. Emily's cries sounded as if they were coming from a person being physically tortured. Robbie, who lived nearby, came right over and held his grief in silent check. Being in Ottawa, Emily managed to get her passport delivered to her for the long fight to San Diego.

Although the thought occurred to Rob that if they didn't go maybe it didn't happen, the next morning they all flew to San Diego. It is certain that morning passed as though it were a nightmare from which they wanted to wake. You can still hear it in Bev's voice. While speaking, her voice would be strong one moment and fade off the next. It was as if she were trying to convince herself that it was true, that three years later she still doesn't quite believe it happened. Yet there she was, on a plane with her grief-stricken husband, remaining son and memories of her oldest baby flooding her tortured mind. Emily, unfortunately, flew in separately from Ottawa.

When they arrived in California, Bev was taken aback by what met them. Immediately upon landing the plane was escorted up to the terminal lined with rows of police vehicles. There stood men and women in uniform waiting to greet them. It was as if that thin blue line could somehow sustain them in their grief, a show of camaraderie and respect from people they had never met. That line was not only trying to hold up the Henwoods, they were hoping that by standing shoulder to shoulder, they could somehow hold each other up. Jeremy Henwood the man wasn't the target, any police officer in uniform was the target. They were all police officers in uniform.

It had really happened, Jeremy was gone. Passengers were asked to remain seated while they exited through a police corridor and waited for Emily to arrive and join them. After a briefing they were escorted to the hospital to meet the doctor and staff that worked on Jeremy. They decided, with the suggestions of staff, that viewing Jeremy would be detrimental and so they lost that simple bit of closure.

As Bev was processing the event in days to come, she kept wondering why people were making such a big deal of Jeremy's death. Why did the video of Jeremy buying a cookie go viral? She couldn't help but think "it was just a cookie." But it was much more than just a cookie.

When a child approaches someone asking for money, it could go one of three ways. The person could ignore the child, he could angrily send them away or, he could give him the ten cents. Jeremy did more than that, he filled a boy's mind and stomach. He spoke to him and treated him kindly. Had Jeremy not died that day, no one would have remembered the cookie.

This happens millions of times throughout the world, kindness toward strangers. What's different is that Jeremy was a police officer, a man society relates to violence, racism, fear and inconvenience. It's a side people forget exists. Officers die on a far too regular basis but their deaths rarely make national news, let alone go viral. Had Jeremy not bought the cookie, few would have remembered his death.

The cookie was the link between being remembered and being forgotten. Jeremy's death enabled people to see that police officers are human. That Jeremy was a man, a soldier, a son, a brother and, a friend. He meant something to many. He was not here to simply walk the earth to be loathed for his chosen profession, none of them are. We can't sacrifice the Jeremy's of the world each time we need to be reminded of this. We need to remember because it matters.

While we are remembering, a family is grieving.

Jeremy's sister Emily had moved back to Ottawa in 2004, fell in love and started a career. Now far from her family, Emily had a difficult time with her brother's death. She had trouble sleeping, lost interest in some of the things she loved and lived with a constant reminder of the fragility of life. She felt guilt over their relationship, wondering if they should have been closer. Because Jeremy was ten years older than Emily, they weren't as close as others. What was a small gap in a relationship became a canyon, and somehow Emily would have to bridge that in her mind so she could focus on the times they had together and the love they shared.

Robbie, an investigator with the Internal Revenue Service, lost his brother and his friend. Robbie had been the one to suggest that Jeremy find safer work with federal law enforcement, he felt that patrolling the streets was becoming too dangerous. He also planned to marry that November with Jeremy as his best man. Rather than celebrating with him he now had make sense of the senseless way his brother was taken.

As the stricter parent, Rob felt he never made amends for the teen-year disputes he had with Jeremy. Every negative interaction came flooding back. He didn't realize that Jeremy had long forgotten, that he had been their cheerleader for many years now. That the love he had bestowed on Jeremy influenced the man he had become.

Bev grieved as only a mother could. Beyond sadness and beyond words. While she was grieving, other families were rejoicing in a bittersweet victory. Jeremy's organs had saved at least two lives.

The first anniversary of Jeremy's death was spent in the Canadian church where Jeremy had been baptized. Although the church had been renovated and expanded over the years, the small chapel remained the same, as if it had been awaiting Jeremy's return. It was a small gathering of people who listened to the Marine Marching Band play "Wind Beneath My Wings" and listen to a reading of "On the Death of the Beloved." In San Diego, there was a large gathering of media, supporters, and the general public raising funds for law enforcement charities. It was a day marked with reflection and respect.

The Henwoods have been to Police Week in Washington, DC twice and return to San Diego regularly. When they returned for the dedication of the Officer Jeremy Henwood Memorial Park across from his midcity division, they were pleased by the memorial marker that bore his name. For them it was "quite amazing."

What was more amazing was the gift they received from his department. They removed Jeremy's locker door signed it, framed it and sent it to the Henwoods. The door was so beautiful that they hung it in the lobby of their clinic. Unfortunately, it wouldn't last long. The door was signed with things such as "end of watch", "see you in the afterlife", "RIP" and "ultimate sacrifice". Despite these etchings, people would ask Bev and Rob, "Got out of the police force, did he? What's he doing now?" Answering these questions became more frustrating as time passed and it was easier to remove the memento.

The locker door is symbolic: it represents the apathy we often see applied to law enforcement. People saw the door, they gave it a cursory glance. They didn't look closely at it, the meaning of what was on the door, or what brought the door there. Eventually the door was removed. This happens all too often with law enforcement. They aren't seen on more than a superficial level, assumptions are made and uninformed questions are asked. I don't want to see a society where they are removed.

The door now resides in a room in the Henwood home, Bev says "Don't expect to go in there and get cheered up. It's a contemplative room." The room is full of the medals and awards that Jeremy received in the Marines and the police department, and mementos from his death.

September 14, 2014 would have been Jeremy's 40th birthday and he may have had children of his own. Instead, his family gathered to remember him. Between tears, his mother read a poem "I'll Lend You a Child" at church. Bev and Rob don't want their oldest son to be forgotten. She wants people to remember what he represented. He was a deep sea rescue diver, a Marine, an officer, an organ donor. He spent time trying to make the lives of poor children better, never lost a man overseas, and he was their son. He led a full life and they are grateful for all of his experiences.

I spoke to Bev as they were packing to leave for their third Concerns of Police Survivors (COPS) Parents Retreat, a place they can go to find comfort and understanding with other families that have lost officers in the line of duty. For them, this retreat is a little easier than others. Bev and Rob have closure, the suspect is dead. Others have to live with the knowledge that the assailant is still free or that they are filing appeal after appeal to regain their freedom. But despite the closure, they will never have their son back.

The killing of a police officer has a ripple effect across the nation, even the world. It's like the wave at a ballgame but you can't see it if you aren't at the game. Every law enforcement family in the world is at the game daily, each officer who falls represents one less person in the stadium. The stadium seems smaller each time. Spouses, children and parents breathe a heavy sigh, a sigh filled with grief for the profession and the fallen. A sigh hiding a smaller one that thinks "Thank God it wasn't mine this time."

That is why the thin blue line is so significant. It's a thread woven through centuries of honor, pride, duty and grief.

Thank you for taking the time to read this book, I hope something here touched your heart or gave you pause. If you are looking for another wonderful book, please consider *Keeping a Blue Light On: A Citizen's Tribute to the Seattle Police Department* by Stacey Sanner. The book is a photo journal with incredible stories and insights from the officers. It was borne from a desire to honor five Seattle-area police officers who were murdered in 2009. Proceeds from the sale of the book benefit the Seattle Police Foundation. Find her at www.keepingabluelighton.com.

Proceeds of this book will be donated to the following charities:

National Law Enforcement Officers Memorial Fund

Founded in 1984, the National Law Enforcement Officers Memorial Fund is dedicated to honoring and remembering the service and sacrifice of law enforcement officers in the United States.

A nonprofit 501(c)(3) organization headquartered in Washington, DC, the Memorial Fund built and continues to maintain the National Law Enforcement Officers Memorial - the nation's monument to law enforcement officers killed in the line of duty. The Memorial Fund is a principal organizer of the National Police Week observance each May and hosts a Candlelight Vigil at the Memorial each May 13th to honor all fallen officers. In addition, the Fund maintains the largest, most comprehensive database of line-of-duty officer deaths, conducts research into officer fatality trends and issues, and serves as an information clearinghouse.

More recently, the Memorial Fund has launched a campaign to build the first-ever National Law Enforcement Museum, adjacent to the Memorial in Washington, DC. The Museum will tell the story of American law enforcement through exhibits, collections, research and education.

Safe Call Now

Safe Call Now is a confidential, comprehensive, 24-hour crisis referral service for all public safety employees, all emergency services personnel and their family members nationwide. Staffed by officers, former law enforcement officers, and public safety professionals; Safe Call Now is a safe place to turn to get help from individuals who understand the demands of a law enforcement career. Safe Call Now provides education, healthy alternatives and resources to save lives and put families back together.

Conferences and training, such as Emotional Body Armor "Breaking Free from the Stigma and Bonds of the Badge", are held throughout the year.

Concerns of Police Survivors (C.O.P.S.)

Each year, between 140 and 160 officers are killed in the line of duty and their families and co-workers are left to cope with the tragic loss. C.O.P.S. provides resources to help them rebuild their shattered lives. There is no membership fee to join C.O.P.S., for the price paid is already too high.

C.O.P.S. was organized in 1984 with 110 individual members. Today C.O.P.S. membership is over 30,000 families. Members include spouses, children, parents, siblings, significant others, and affected co-workers of officers killed in the line of duty according to Federal government criteria. C.O.P.S. is governed by a National Board of law enforcement survivors. All programs and services are administered by the National Office in Camdenton, Missouri. C.O.P.S. has over 50 Chapters nationwide that work with survivors at the grass-roots level.

C.O.P.S. programs for survivors include the National Police Survivors' Conference held each May during National Police Week, scholarships, peer-support at the national, state, and local levels, "C.O.P.S. Kids" counseling reimbursement program, the "C.O.P.S. Kids" Summer Camp, "C.O.P.S. Teens" Outward Bound experience for young adults, special retreats for spouses, parents, siblings, adult children, in-laws, and co-workers, trial and parole support, and other assistance programs.

PoliceWives.org

PoliceWives is a national nonprofit group established in 2002 for the support of LEO's and their families. They are a unique group consisting of women & men from all walks of life, who share a common bond of having a loved one in law enforcement.

In addition to their extensive support forums, throughout the year members take part in many activities designed to provide support to other site members as well as the law enforcement community as a whole. PoliceWives raises money to purchase bullet proof vests for canine officers; through "Baby Blue" blankets and stuffed animals are collected and sent to departments in need of such items and; members may request aid for themselves or for an officer/family within their own police dept. To qualify for aid, the applicant must be affected by a serious, terminal, or life-threatening injury or illness that has altered their current living situation to the point that assistance would be a relief.

ABOUT THE AUTHOR

Karen Solomon is a graduate of Eckerd College and blogs as The Missing Niche. Her writing has been featured on PoliceMag.com and To Write Love on Her Arms. She lives in New England with her husband, 2 children and 2 dogs.

JUL 2015

Riverhead Free Library
330 Court Street
Riverhead, New York 11901

9 780986 322105